Limitless Women

CHARTING THE PATH TO UNSTOPPABLE SUCCESS

Published by Game Changer Publishing

Paperback ISBN: 978-1-965653-48-7

Hardcover ISBN: 978-1-965653-49-4

Digital ISBN: 978-1-965653-50-0

www.GameChangerPublishing.com

Contents

Foreword

In business, there are very few books that spark an actual movement. Limitless Women is one of those books. It's a manifesto, a rallying cry for every woman who's ever been told to "stay in her lane" or that her dreams were impossible. This book will inspire you to know and believe that there are no limits.

Women are at the forefront of change across industries, from boardrooms to classrooms to courtrooms, yet the path to true empowerment is often flooded with self-doubt, fear, and a lack of confidence. *Limitless Women* doesn't just give you permission to break free from the "norm" —it hands you the keys to the kingdom. Within the pages of this book, you will meet visionary women who have shattered glass ceilings, pushed boundaries, and redefined success. But more than just stories, this book offers actionable strategies that will enable you to do the same.

What makes *Limitless Women* truly powerful is that it's not just for those on the cusp of greatness—it's for every woman, whether you're already making waves or just beginning to tap into your potential. This book will show you that it's never too late, too early, or impossible to claim the life you desire.

The words here aren't just meant to inspire; they are a call to action. You'll be challenged to rethink what's holding you back, confront the fear that's keeping you small, and harness the power of your intuition and resilience to build a life that's not only successful but limitless.

You are about to embark on a journey of transformation. After reading this book, you will be stronger, inspired, more confident, and most importantly, unafraid to stand in your own greatness and who you were really called to be.

Remember that the world needs your voice, your ideas, and your leadership, and this book is your guide, your permission slip, and your inspiration. The time has come to step into your limitless potential!

With gratitude and belief,

Cris Cawley

Mindset Reset

UNLOCKING YOUR PATH TO ABUNDANCE AND SUCCESS

By Anna Pexa

Hello, everyone. I am Anna Pexa, a 47-year-old mompreneur and registered nurse from the Midwest. My husband and I have been married for 22 years, and we have an amazing family with three kids. My life can be a little crazy at times, but I would not trade it for anything. My three kids keep me very busy. Watching them grow into amazing humans is so rewarding. So often, I felt like a failure as a mom. Can you relate? Seeing my kids succeed lets me know I did not fail as a mom. My daughter is twenty and is in college, studying nursing. She is passionate about acting and enjoys doing color guard in the marching band. My middle child is seventeen and is a senior in high school. Bring on the mom's tears. He loves playing football and wrestling. My youngest is in eighth grade. He also enjoys football and has recently taken up wrestling. Wrestling might be his new passion. Balancing parenthood, running a business, and working full-time as a nurse can be challenging. It takes a lot of mindset work and being consistent. Being organized is a must. In this chapter, I will share how changing my mindset transformed my life, from filing bankruptcy twice to earning over six figures. If I can change my story, you can too.

My journey to where I am today has been a long, winding road filled with many obstacles. I grew up poor, though I did not think about it then. I was raised by a single mom who was my rock. She got to play the role of mom and dad all in one. I never really knew my parents together. They divorced when I was young. I did not know any different. My dad was not around, and though I tried to convince myself it did not affect me, years of self-sabotage and feeling unworthy showed me otherwise. I eventually realized that my past mattered more than I wanted to admit. I began to understand how deeply my past influenced my present. That was when I realized that things needed to change. It is not always easy and takes a lot of daily work. However, if this poor girl from the trailer park can do it, you can too. My goal is to help other women know their worth. No one should ever have to live life feeling unworthy. God made us with a purpose, and he has plans for us. It is time we stepped into who we are meant to be.

The purpose of this chapter is so other women can see that they do have a purpose and do not have to suffer as long as I did. I know I have succeeded if I can help one mompreneur find her way without feeling lost. Being a mompreneur can be a challenging and lonely road. I spent years going through the motions, living numb, pouring everything into my kids while neglecting myself. Can you relate? Looking back, I was likely a little depressed and did not even realize it. Everything started to shift once I started working on myself and filling my cup first. My passion is to help other moms do the same.

If you are a busy mompreneur trying to survive, this chapter is for you. I have been in your shoes, just going through the motions. It is time that you start to thrive. I am here to help you learn how to go from "hot mess express" to "Boss Mom" success—leaving the hustle train behind and getting you back in the driver's seat of your life so you can thrive. I have spent a lot of time and money to break through my glass ceiling, and now I am sharing what I have learned to help other moms shift from survival mode to thriving.

You can learn how to go from merely surviving to thriving. Mindset is the key to getting yourself unstuck. There are a few different types of mindsets. We will focus on having a growth mindset and living an abundant life with a positive money mindset. We are going to promote growth and abundance. You will learn how to overcome the obstacles that may come your way. Trust me, you will come up against obstacles, and being prepared for them will set you up for success. Mindset is the key to success. As American industrialist and business magnate Henry Ford said, "Whether you think you can or think you can't, you're right." You get to choose your reality. What will you choose?

THE IMPORTANCE OF MINDSET

Mindset is crucial to success in both your personal and professional life. We will learn how to shift from a poverty mindset to an abundance mindset. Mindset has the power to shape your reality. I spent years believing I was not smart enough, worthy enough, pretty enough, or skinny enough to be successful. I was just going through the motions and never finding true happiness. Have you ever felt that way? Discovering the importance of mindset was a total game-changer for me. It was a concept not taught in school or even by my mom but something I stumbled upon through network marketing. It took years to work through my baggage, and I still have things I work on daily. I tend to slip back into old patterns if I do not prioritize my mindset. One piece of advice from me to you is *do not compare your chapter one to my chapter one*. We all have different journeys and life circumstances that have brought us to where we are now. What takes me three years might take you one, or it could take ten, and that is okay. It is your journey and yours alone. Do not give up on yourself; people are counting on you to fulfill your life's purpose so they can live out their purpose. You matter!

GET UNSTUCK

The first step to getting unstuck is identifying what is holding you back. Do not rush this process. Uncovering the triggers that keep you stuck will take some soul-searching. The events in your life that have hidden themselves away creep up without you even realizing it. Awareness is going to be critical. You will have to own your circumstances. You have the power to rewrite your story. No one else has the power to write your story unless you let them. It is your time to shine. Dig deep to understand why you feel stuck and/or frustrated. The hardest thing I had to do was admit that I was the one holding myself back. It was not my work, my network marketing company, my husband, or my family, but me. The first step is realizing you hold the key to moving forward. It is time for you to take back control of your life!

To help you figure out your sabotaging traits, I offer free training called Unleashing Your Inner Champion: Overcome Imposter Syndrome, Limiting Beliefs, and Self-Sabotage. You can find it on my website. It is an excellent add-on to this chapter. Once you identify what is holding you back, it becomes easier to move forward. Learn to recognize your triggers for self-sabotaging. Typical forms of self-sabotage include procrastination, perfectionism, negative self-talk, fear of failure or success, and setting unrealistic goals. Once you recognize these behaviors, you can change your mindset and set yourself up for the success you deserve.

GROWTH MINDSET

A growth mindset is the belief that your abilities can improve through effort, learning, and persistence. You can apply a growth mindset in any aspect of your life, from your career to your business, hobbies, and more. It is the belief that you can always grow through learning, hard work, and dedication. It just takes shifting from a fixed mindset, believing you cannot change your circumstances, to a growth mindset. Think you are worthy of success and happiness.

MONEY/ABUNDANCE

An abundance mindset is the belief that there is plenty of everything in the world. Plenty of happiness, joy, resources, money, wealth, customers, and more exist. Living with an abundance mindset means you do not worry about competition. You believe there is more than enough to go around. For example, if you sell health and wellness products, you do not worry about competing with others because you know plenty of customers are out there. You will attract the right people to you. Living an abundant life means viewing life through the lens of gratitude.

Your money mindset is your set of beliefs surrounding money. Do you have a positive or negative mindset about money? Your beliefs influence managing debt, saving money, and spending money. I grew up poor and unknowingly struggled with a scarcity mindset for many years. I could never get ahead, no matter how hard I worked. The more money I would make, the more money I would spend. Can you relate? It is the reason I filed for bankruptcy not once but twice. Filing bankruptcy is my little secret that I have not discussed for years. Something I thought I would never share. However, if I can help one person, it is worth sharing. I learned things the hard way. My goal is to help others not have to learn the same way. A poor money mindset is something I struggle with, and I work on it daily. The good news is that you can change your money mindset with hard work, just like I have. Daily mindset work is essential.

Many people struggle with negative feelings about money. I remember hearing people talk negatively about "rich" people, calling them conceited. I truly thought having a lot of money would make me conceited. These kinds of thoughts can hold you back from your true potential. A poor money mindset can affect your emotions and how you manage money, leading to feelings of shame, stress, fear, guilt, or fear of what others will think. These negative emotions can make you feel like you are not good with money. This leads to a self-fulfilling prophecy where you unconsciously make poor choices that keep you stuck in negative financial situations.

A poor money mindset can cause limiting beliefs like *I do not deserve wealth* or *Money is the root of all evil.* These beliefs can prevent you from pursuing opportunities, asking for raises, or seeking career growth. You might fear failure, which keeps you in your comfort zone and limits your potential for financial growth and success. A poor money mindset can prevent you from attracting and retaining wealth. Being unable to attract and retain wealth can lead to missed opportunities, stagnant income, and limited financial success. Overcoming these obstacles starts with recognizing and changing your beliefs and attitudes about money.

A positive money mindset can lead to greater financial freedom, stability, and success.

Having a poor money mindset often stems from various life experiences. For me, it started in childhood. Being raised by a single mom, money was tight, leading me to believe that money is hard to come by. When I had an overabundance, I spent it because I did not think I deserved savings. I didn't feel worthy of financial stability. Cultural and societal influences also influence our beliefs, such as rich people being the root of all evil or rich people being conceited. Having negative thoughts about money can cause you to feel guilty about wanting more money or lead to an aversion to wealth. Traumatic financial events like losing a job, debt, or bankruptcy can also negatively impact your money mindset, causing anxiety and fear.

Negative self-talk reinforces a poor money mindset, such as telling yourself you're not good with money or that you'll never be financially stable. Negative thoughts about money can lead to a cycle where you make poor financial choices, keeping you stuck. I did this for years without even realizing it. The good news is that it's never too late to unlearn a poor money mindset and change your view on money.

HOW TO OVERCOME A POOR MONEY MINDSET

A poor money mindset and a scarcity mentality often go hand in hand. It creates a vicious cycle of fear and limitation that can be tough to break. The good news is that with intention and consistent effort, you can shift these beliefs and open yourself to abundance. Next, we will cover how to break free from the chains of a poor money mindset.

STEP 1: IDENTIFY YOUR TRIGGERS AND SELF-SABOTAGING BEHAVIORS

The first step is to identify your triggers and recognize how you might be self-sabotaging your financial growth. You can use my free self-sabotage workbook and the video to guide you. See my webpage link at the end of this chapter for the free training. Begin reflecting on your thoughts and beliefs around money. Be brutally honest with yourself;

growth requires it. Begin journaling your specific thoughts around money. Whenever you feel anxious or have negative thoughts, write them down. Over time, you'll notice patterns and underlying beliefs that might hold you back. Once we identify your beliefs around money, we can work on turning those beliefs around.

STEP 2: CHALLENGE YOUR LIMITING BELIEFS

Once you've identified your limiting beliefs, it's time to challenge them. Ask yourself, *Is this belief true? Is this how God sees me? What evidence do I have to support this belief?* Often, you'll find that these beliefs are based on assumptions and not facts. You can develop a more positive and empowering money mindset by questioning and reframing these thoughts.

STEP 3: SHIFT FROM SCARCITY TO ABUNDANCE

Shifting from a scarcity mindset to an abundance mindset requires focusing on what you have rather than what you lack. An abundance mindset is about believing there is enough to go around and that you can attract wealth. Start by practicing daily gratitude. Begin your day by listing at least three things you are grateful for, especially about finances. It can be as simple as appreciating that you can pay your bills or have a roof over your head. Over time, this practice will shift your mindset from scarcity to abundance.

STEP 4: PAIR YOUR MINDSET SHIFTS WITH ACTION

Mindset shifts are powerful, but you must pair them with action steps. Start by setting financial goals that reflect your new, empowered beliefs about money. Begin with baby steps, like saving a small amount each month. For example, I started by putting money into my savings account and leaving a more significant chunk in my checking account so I could get used to seeing a larger balance without spending it. Initially, seeing a large amount in my checking account was tough. I wanted to spend it. But now, I can shift more into savings without hesitation. My husband likes to save spare change, including dollar bills and fives. We have an envelope for our dollar bills and a jar for the change. It is nice to have for a rainy day or vacation. This small habit has proven helpful during unexpected expenses. As you align your actions with your new abundance mindset, create a financial plan that includes short-term and long-term goals. Break these goals down into actionable steps. It is important to celebrate your small victories along the way. Celebrating your small wins will reinforce your new mindset.

SURROUND YOURSELF WITH POSITIVE INFLUENCES

Another essential step in changing your mindset is surrounding yourself with others who have a positive outlook and are where you want to be. Who we surround ourselves with impacts our mindset positively and negatively. Choose people who will help grow your abundance mindset. Seek out communities, both in person and online, that support your growth. I find much support in my church group and Facebook groups with other like-minded women. Surrounding yourself with mentors and friends who have a healthy relationship with money and inspire you to think bigger is essential. Joining a mastermind group focused on a money mindset, financial growth, or an abundance mentality can be incredibly beneficial.

CREATE A ROUTINE THAT WORKS FOR YOU

Changing your money mindset doesn't happen overnight. It requires patience, persistence, and daily effort. There will be times when old patterns resurface, but remember, this is a journey, not a destination.

A couple of years ago, I discovered *The Miracle Morning* by Hal Elrod, a game changer. I teach this in my challenges and coaching programs. How you start your day sets the tone for your entire day. The Miracle Morning routine uses the SAVERS acronym Silence (meditation, prayer), Affirmations, Visualization, Exercise, Reading, and Journaling. This routine doesn't have to be done in the morning; you can fit it into your day as it works for you. For example, I start my day with silence, prayers, and time with God, then head to the gym. I practice affirmations during breaks at work and do my reading, scribing (journaling), and visualization at night. The key is to create a routine that fits your schedule and stick to it. Don't let your schedule be your excuse to stay stuck. When there is a will, there is a way.

HOW TO HANDLE OPPOSITION AND SELF-SABOTAGE

As you grow and evolve in your mindset, it's not uncommon for opposition and self-sabotage to come into play. Your old self may cling on for dear life, resisting the change. Your ego feels safe in your old self and will do whatever it takes to try and hold you back. The resistance means you are on the right path. Keep pushing forward; a breakthrough is about to happen.

Opposition can come from others or from within. Not everyone will understand your journey or want to support your growth. Some may feel threatened or uncomfortable because your change highlights their stagnation. It's essential not to take other people's opinions personally. Focus on what is best for you. Surround yourself with those who genuinely support your journey. When opposition comes from within, it usually manifests as doubt or fear. Acknowledge it, but don't let it control you. Use it to refine your goals, strengthen your resolve, and push forward.

Self-sabotage is tricky and often subtle. Most people don't even realize they are doing it. It can show up as procrastination, negative self-talk, or making excuses for why you can't achieve your goal. One of the lessons I have learned along the way is to take ownership. It would help if you became aware of your patterns of self-sabotage. You need to acknowledge them and use the tools you are learning to continue to move forward. My freebie on self-sabotage can help you identify your self-sabotage traits. Pay attention to when and how they show up. Write them down. Write how you feel and what helped you work through these self-sabotaging traits. Are you avoiding tasks that are crucial for your growth? Are you telling yourself you're not good enough? Once you are aware, challenge these thoughts and behaviors. Remind yourself why you're doing this in the first place. If you don't have a strong *why,* it's time to figure out what it is. My free training on discovering your why can help you uncover your why. Go seven layers deep. Replace negative self-talk with affirmations that align with your new mindset.

Some people in your circle will grow with you, and others will not. It's okay to walk away from toxic or negative influences. We think we can't walk away from negative or toxic people. However, Jesus did! Walking away from those who want to hold you back or treat you poorly is okay. More than two dozen times in the four gospels, Jesus walked away from others or let others walk away from him. *"If anyone will not welcome you or listen to your words, leave that home or town and shake the dust off your feet"* (Matthew 10:14). Building and growing healthy support networks are essential.

In this chapter, we have reviewed how you can shift your mindset and transform your life. We have looked into the importance of mindset, gone over ways to get unstuck, and discussed how to cultivate a growth and abundance mindset. We have also discussed the challenges of overcoming a poor money mindset. Next, we covered the importance of surrounding yourself with like-minded and positive people to help you continue to grow your mindset.

Thank you so much for taking the time to read my chapter. It means so much that you invest in yourself and your future. I hope you walk away from this chapter with the resources you need to help you feel empowered and inspired to make changes to live a life of abundance and purpose.

Your journey is your journey. The possibilities are endless. You have it in you to make your dreams come true. The power is within you to rewrite your story. God wants you to live out your purpose and live abundantly. It is time for you to get excited about what is possible because, with the right mindset and God on your side, there is nothing you cannot accomplish.

If you loved what you learned in this chapter and want to learn more, connect with me on social media, visit my website, and schedule your free discovery call to see how I can help you continue to move forward in your journey to success. If you book a free discovery call with me and mention this book, you will get a free social media mastery, free social media audit, free Trello content planner board, and free Trello 30 days' worth of content board.

Anna Pexa is an RN, MSN, social media and Mindset coach, and published author. She is also a mom, wife, and strong-willed Christian woman! She loves to show mompreneurs how to take God along on their business adventures. She also loves showing mompreneurs how to get off the hustle train back into the driver's seat to move out of survival mode into thriving mode.

If you're ready to take the next step in building your business with faith and purpose, head over to my website for more ways we can work together and start seeing the results you've been praying for! Let's Make it Happen!

For more information or to reach Anna
https://annapexa.com/

—

Facebook
https://www.facebook.com/anna.pexa27/

—

Instagram
https://www.instagram.com/anna.pexa27/

—

TikTok
@annapexa

The Future is Psychic

UNDERSTANDING THE UNIVERSAL LANGUAGE

By Carrie Cardozo

Like most people in life, I was born a psychic, but unlike others, I never forgot my gifts or stopped using them. I never really knew that who I was or what I was doing would result in the power and accuracy that I have today. I'm a master psychic, healer, and energy worker, and for the longest time, I didn't know that what I did was any different from anyone else. My first recollection of communicating with spirits was at about the age of two. I didn't know it at the time, as I thought the beings I saw and the energy I felt around me were all in my head. At least, that's what my mom always told me. I would tell her about the lady in the attic, and she assumed I was pretending. I'd tell her about the spirits I saw, and half the time, she said it was just a dream. I'd tell people what I knew about a person and was told it was only my opinion. You see, as a child, I could see spirits. I could read energetics, and I could see future events. I knew people better than they knew themselves. I could see what they had done, how they felt, and if they were lying or not.

I grew up thinking everyone else experienced life the same way until my life started unfolding just like I had seen as a child. From divorces to births to cancer, I witnessed each event in great detail in visions as a child. It made me start questioning everything. I asked others if this happened to them and no one else had experienced it. I started to question all the things that had happened, and each time, I found an excuse or a reason as to why I might have "imagined" my future the exact way it had unfolded. I didn't want to admit or believe that I was psychic.

Then, in 2014, when I was running a multi-million dollar company, raising three amazing kids, and building a future with the man of my dreams, tragedy struck, and my gifts were undeniable. I found my partner unresponsive in our living room, and later that day, he was pronounced dead. The days that followed were the hardest and most heart-shattering times of my life as I tried to understand what happened and why. In the deepest moments of my sadness and sorrow, I could feel him still there. In the moments of a total loss of control over my emotions, I'd feel this settling of calmness and reassurance. There was this need to know where he went and how to connect with him. I needed answers to life's biggest questions, and suddenly, that seemed the only thing that was important to me. In the weeks that followed, those pockets of calmness and peace that took over my whole body got stronger and stronger, and the feeling of his presence kept getting more tangible till I started to see and hear him. I could feel his presence whenever he was around. I could hear messages. I knew what he was trying to tell me, and my realizations of who I was and what I was able to do came flooding in.

I was psychic. I could tap into the energy, see the unseen, hear the messages, see the future, and know the energetic truth of anything I dug into. I very quickly realized the importance of who I was and what I was here to do. I started practicing my gifts, unlocking more and more psychic skills as my connection grew deeper and deeper. In October 2014, the business that I had been running for several years collapsed, and I walked out of that office knowing it was time to use my gifts and start living my true purpose. I realized the power of my gifts and the importance of what my abilities offered so many people, from healing to deeper soul connection to helping people build and grow businesses that impact the world and bring great amounts of wealth. My life completely changed because of accepting and using my gifts. The world is clearer; I understand people and situations better, the path to take has been made clear, and the way in which my gifts help to transform other people's lives is incomparable.

I've spent the last seven years of my life activating psychic gifts in hundreds of my clients, some of my friends, and even my children, and I've never failed. I have a 100 percent activation success rate because it's aligned with our journey here as a soul. I'd like to take you on this journey deep into the psychic energy to understand it, accept it, and start to welcome it into your life. I'm going to help you see how you are already psychic and how you use your abilities without even knowing it, and then I'm going to help you see the power in the gifts that you hold. Every single person is psychic. It's something we are born with. But when we come into this life, we forget who we really are. We lose our connection back to truth and we start living a life that others have impressed upon us. A life where we are told what to think, how to live, what to do, what's right, and how to be accepted into society. And it causes us to lose connection to ourselves. But opening up your psychic gifts allows you to see the truth of life and to live your life on your terms in a way you never realized existed.

The future is psychic, and I believe that every single person has the ability to open and use their psychic gifts to enhance and transform their life. My psychic abilities and communication with spirits have allowed me to understand what happens on the other side. We can get a clear understanding and confirmation as to our true purpose here in this life. One thing has been made incredibly clear: We have come to Earth, into this life, to remember who we are and to realize our connection back to Source/God/Allah/Oneness/Divine (for the purpose of this chapter, I'll refer to this higher power as Source). We're here to connect to the world on an energetic level and expand our consciousness beyond recognition of the life we know now. I have come to realize that the life we see, the one we experience day after day, is clouded by our traumas, our limitations, and the past that has kept us stuck and limited. Activating your psychic gifts shifts your entire reality and opens you to see and experience life how you were meant to, through the lens of energetics.

We live in a world of energetics and are tapping into it at every moment, even when we are not conscious of it. Energetics are all around you. In everything you see, everything you touch, every word you communicate. You're feeling it even when you aren't able to understand it. Ever walk into a room and immediately feel like something bad is going on? Ever had a specific feeling about someone you just met? Ever feel that rush of joy that runs through your body at something exciting? Ever think about someone, and then, out of the blue, they call? That's you connecting to the energetic vibration of something. Every single thing holds what we call an energetic vibration, and each one is a very specific and unique vibration that allows us to identify what it is. This vibration is similar to a fingerprint or a signature. When you feel it or see it, you immediately understand it. This energetic vibration is the language of the unseen. We call it the "Universal Language" because every single person—no matter what language they speak, even aliens, if you believe in them ;-)—understands the language of energetics. The language of energetics is different from the spoken or written word in that it's always true. Energetic can't be faked. The energy will always reveal to you what it really is. So, the energy of joy will always hold the exact same vibration. The energy of fear holds a very specific yet different vibration. Just like the written language, if you see the word "cat," you're always going to think of a cat. If you see a specific vibration, you'll know exactly what it means.

People often refer to reading energetics as using their intuition, and this is partially correct. You can use your intuition to read energetics, but most often, you are using your psychic abilities. There is a difference between intuition and psychic abilities, and lots of times it's misunderstood. Intuition is connecting and reading energetics that lie inside oneself, while psychic abilities connect to and read the energetics outside of oneself. The communication of energetics as a psychic is not just reading the energy. It's being able to communicate with spirits. It's looking into the past or the future. It's talking to the souls of any living thing. It's about being able to understand or communicate with anything in life.

We have been taught that intuition is something that everyone has and that psychic abilities are only for people who are special. But in truth, everyone has both. People have misunderstood what psychic means for centuries. Even the Cambridge definition of psychic is as follows:

Psychic /'saɪkɪk/ A person who has a special mental ability, for example, being able to know what will happen in the future or what people are thinking: a gifted psychic.

People mistake the reading of energetics and intuition for something that is connected to the mind. But neither of them is a mind function. I've heard people teach that your intuition is in your subconscious, but that is not true at all. Reading energetics, or using your psychic or intuitive abilities, is connecting to the energetic vibration and understanding truth. To do this, we must leave the mind out of it. The mind isn't involved in connecting to energy. The mind houses your ego, which is programmed to keep you safe. Your mind is also where your past, your experiences, your knowledge, and your wisdom are stored. Everything you believe, everything you think, every desire, all of your opinions. Now imagine if all of this was caught up in you trying to interpret the truth of energy. You'd never see the truth. You'd never be able to accurately read the energy. You'd try to solve it instead of hearing it. You'd try to reason or logic your way to the answer.

Your intuition and your psychic abilities and connections are stored in your heart space. They are at the seat of your soul. They are in the center of your chest, deep within your higher heart chakra, where the true energetics of who you are, as well as your connection back to Source, lies. This is where the intuition, the knowing of your own truth, of your own path, of what feels good and aligned for you, is stored. And this is also where the psychic connection and the ability to read energetics in all aspects of life lies.

We are born into this life connected at various levels to our intuition and our psychic gifts. We understand energetics, and we know why we are here and what our path in life is going to look like. Some very connected children also remember their past life as well. But as we grow and as we are taught to learn a desired curriculum, as we are impressed upon by society and family, as we build fears, limiting beliefs, and opinions, that connection is overpowered and silenced by the mind, and we think we lose our connection. Most people aren't conscious of this connection. They aren't actively reading energetics because they aren't tapped into their intuition or psychic abilities. It's not lost. It's waiting for you to reactivate it. Most people never lose their intuition; they just don't often follow it. Your intuition is always within. You're more connected to the energetics inside of you, so most often, people use their intuition without even knowing it. Being psychic is very different. It's connecting to the energy that can have no relation to you; it has no impact on your energetics and so you lose touch very quickly in life. People who are psychic are not special. They are not different from others in any way except that they never lose that connection for many different reasons, or they reach the point in their life where it is time to awaken their gifts.

Psychic abilities can open up when you reach a very specific point in your soul journey. This journey can be a specific event, like the passing of my partner, or it can be a pull from within that urges you to look deeper into truths and universal understanding. It can happen when there is a traumatic event, an accident, a near-death experience, or even what others relate to as a "dark night of the soul" where everything in your life is coming apart to awaken your truth. When this happens, there is a shedding that must unfold. That shedding involves deep inner healing, the release of mind control, a strong connection to oneself, and a journey into truth. You are forced to live life differently. You're asked to get deeply connected to your soul and start to live a more conscious life on the path of ascension.

Not everyone has to have a traumatic event to signify the opening of their psychic journey and gifts. People can also get signs that it's time. These signs can come from the spirit or can come from your body. Spirit is always speaking to you. But the more tapped in and farther along on your journey, the more you'll see them. These signs often come in threes and can be repeating numbers, animal visits, or certain objects like a rainbow, hearts, or butterflies. They can also be certain phrases or things people keep saying to you that resonate with your intuition as a message of deeper connection.

As the time comes for you to activate and use your psychic abilities, you can also get signs from your own body. From ringing in the ears to dizzy headaches to changes in your vision. Some people become ultra-sensitive to touch, smells, or specific things. This is how your body starts to open up what we call "psychic channels." Channels are the way in which you connect to energy outside of yourself. It's how you read and interpret energetics. You can also often get sick when you start to activate your abilities. Activating your abilities requires a shift in your own internal energetic vibration. We call it raising your vibration. In order to raise your vibration, you have to release the negative, heavy vibrations you're holding onto, i.e., fear, anger, trauma, and limiting beliefs. If you do that, it might cause you to get a cold, get a stomach bug, or experience anything that allows your body to physically release the old energy you are storing.

Whether you're aware of it or not, your psychic gifts are unfolding all the time, some at a faster rate than others. What I love is when I help people realize that they are already tapping in, using their gifts, and they don't even realize it. I see a lot of things that people pass off as a coincidence or not real that are clear indications of psychic gifts. Like when you see orbs with your physical eyes, you can rest assured they are spirits. When you see sparkling lights or quick flashes of lights, those are normally angels. When you see dark shadows in your peripheral vision, those are most often departed loved ones. Right before sleep or right before waking up (twilight), you will start to hear words like your name being called or have a specific word stuck in your head. That is a spirit trying to talk to you. You might see specific images in your head or in your third eye that come out of nowhere. You'll see things in your life unfold. You'll start to have answers to questions you know nothing about. You'll have a sense of knowing that goes far beyond the intellectual understanding that you hold. These are all ways that spirit and energetics communicate with you and all ways that show you that you really are psychic.

I had a client who came to me because she desired to heal on a deeper level from a life of trauma and abuse. We started off with healing work and connecting her back to her soul. In less than two sessions together, two hours, she realized that she was psychic. I showed her that many of the things she was experiencing were really her guides trying to communicate with her. She had been filled with anxiety, having trouble sleeping, and waking up at 2 a.m. every morning with racing thoughts. When she would awaken, she would feel like there was a male presence in the room. I connected her to her guide and helped her to understand the message and what she had been thinking. All that had been in her head was exactly what the guides told us. She now uses her psychic abilities in her business and her life, and things have become so different for her.

When you use your gifts and abilities in life, it's like you are living only half of your reality. It's like living life in a very dimly lit room, trying to find your way around and figure out where everything is; then someone switches on the light, and everything becomes crystal clear and focused. People often think that psychic abilities are for communicating with the dead, telling the future, and sharing bits of past lives. They are, but what's even more powerful than that is using psychic abilities in everything you do. For example, in the day-to-day things that you don't even think about, you wish someone else would make some decisions in the areas of your life. One of my least favorite parts of my day is figuring out what I should wear. So one day I asked my guides, and I saw the outfit in my head. Do you know how many compliments I had on that outfit? I'm a busy, single mom of three, and the last thing I want to do at the end of the day is figure out what's for dinner. I use my guides for that now. I have clients who use the energy to determine what foods work best for them, clients who choose which books to read, and clients who use guides to figure out where to travel and what route to take.

You might be asking yourself, *What restaurant is most aligned? Which order should I run errands in?* The energetics and the guides know best, and if you're connected, aligned with the vibration, and listening, you'll always understand what is best for you. One time, I was booking a flight, and for logistical purposes, I wanted to leave at 2 p.m. It would have gotten me into my location earlier in the evening so I could have dinner with my daughter. Every time I went to book the flight, I heard *No.* My card was declined, or the website would freeze. I tuned in, asked why, and kept hearing *5 p.m.* But my mind didn't want 5 p.m. That would get me there at midnight, and that felt exhausting. Now, I know that my mind never knows best, but my psychic abilities do. I booked the 5 p.m. flight. On the day of the flight, we had a blizzard. The airport was shut down till 4 p.m. So, my flight was one of the first to leave that day. If I hadn't listened, I would never have made that flight.

I don't just use my abilities to make decisions for myself; I use them for help in parenting, in relationships, and in my friendships, too. As a parent, there are so many things that can unfold that are unexpected and often stressful. Navigating trying to raise another human while you are attempting to experience your own life can be supported and made easier by your psychic gifts. The energy is going to tell you what's most aligned for your child. It's going to help you understand what they are going through, and you can absolutely tell when they are lying. But navigating that dynamic between knowing everything as a parent and supporting your own child's journey is key.

Remember, we come into this life with a connection back to Source that can either be fostered or shut down. When you're tapped into your psychic abilities, you have the advantage of supporting your own child's gifts. You can support them in their connection and also their journey. Just like you, your child came here to experience life. That means all the good and the bad things that you experience; your child has a whole bunch of their own. But this isn't easy for parents to navigate. Parents want to shield and protect their children and make sure not a single bad thing happens. Although we are supposed to keep our kids safe, we are also supposed to help them to experience their own journey in life so that they, too keep evolving as a soul. When you are tapped into your psychic abilities and you're understanding what your child is experiencing and why, you become the ultimate support.

I had a client who was having some pretty rough times with her teen daughter, from skipping school to getting in fights to stealing her grandma's credit card and charging things she wasn't supposed to. The mother was overwhelmed, stressed out, and at her wit's end dealing with her daughter all on her own as she was estranged from her daughter's father. Tapping into the energetics, she was able to see that trying to make her daughter change and trying to control everything she did wasn't going to work because she needed to experience these things, feel the discomfort, and learn from the lessons. She also saw that it was important for her father to be back in her life. The mom switched how she was parenting. She released her need to have her daughter a certain way. She shifted her relationship with the father, and in less than four months, everything changed. The father was back in her life and co-parenting so beautifully, and the daughter's behavior drastically shifted.

Not only did this client use her abilities to shift the direction of her daughter's life, but she also was able to mend a relationship with a man who was important in her and her daughter's life. Her abilities allowed her to understand where he was coming from, to see what was needed to allow him to feel welcome and important in their life, and taught her how to navigate co-parenting in a way that everyone wins! It's one of my favorite success stories!

There isn't an area of life in which you can't use your psychic abilities, but my favorite place to use them besides teaching others is in business. When talking to spirits and souls on the other side, I am constantly given the message that you are here for a purpose and to share that with the world.

Your business, most often, is a pathway to share your purpose with the world. It's the place you get to show up and shine. You get to be the most beautiful expression of who you are, and reaching new levels of success and new levels of impact grows exponentially when you use your psychic gifts. I use my psychic abilities in all aspects of my business. Whether it's for my own business growth or for assisting others in building a business that gives them freedom of time and money and rapid expansion, it is the fastest way to align your offers, your message, and your prices with what your desired clients and audience are going to align with. That allows you to get more sales in a shorter amount of time. Tapping into the energy allows you to see what your clients need most, how to deliver that to them, and what price you are going to sell that offer at. I see a lot of people who create things that aren't aligned, and when they go to sell them, it's a flop. That doesn't happen when you use your psychic abilities.

Business isn't just about you or your clients; it's also about the team you put together and how efficiently and harmoniously everything runs. When you are psychic you have the ability to tap into the energetics and the truth that lies inside each of your team members. You can see their strengths and weaknesses and know exactly where they are going to serve the best inside your business. You can do the same with partnerships, collaborations, as well as opportunities that unexpectedly show up at your door. Everything can sound great on the outside, but when you know the energetics and you use your abilities, you get confirmation that it's what is going to be the biggest asset and success for your business. Your relationships with employees will improve and the harmony and connection you get with your clients and partners will be the most aligned and beneficial.

I had a client hire me to help expand his business. He was looking for an investor in the realm of several hundred million dollars. He asked me to look at the relationship, the connection, and the potential success of the partnership that was offered to him. When I did, I could see very clearly that the investor did not have the same ethics or values that my client did and that his business dealings were not always ethical. I was also able to see that the future for this investor was not looking very good and that something was going to happen. I shared with my client what I had seen in relation to the deal and advised him not to take the offer. Five months later, the investor was arrested for fraud.

In business, we can often make decisions that look good on paper and have all the metrics to back them up, but that doesn't always mean it's a great opportunity for us. Without energetics and your psychic abilities, you're driven by your own biases, mood, or external factors, often leading to things that don't work out the way you want them to. Or they might lead to great success but at the sacrifice of your values or health. When you use your psychic abilities, you tap into alignment with your soul. You know what is going to feel good, give you more of what you are looking for, and achieve the goals and success you desire.

Every person has come into this life to leave a soul-aligned impact on the world, but many people struggle to understand exactly what that impact is. When you have opened your psychic abilities, when you are tapped into energetics, and when you are making decisions that are driven by the information you are receiving in the energetics, you fulfill that purpose.

Imagine if life could really be simplified and made even more fulfilling by accessing something that is held deep within. A life that holds a harmonious family, a relationship that is fulfilling, and a business that is thriving. Yes, you'll have the benefits of money and success, but most importantly, it's the impact and growth of your soul that completely changes your life.

My psychic gifts have transformed my life in ways that are hard to even explain. I went from being a broken, lost business executive to having the life that I never thought was possible by using my psychic gifts. But part of our purpose in being here is to activate new levels of personal power and those levels include your psychic gifts. As much as I love being psychic and doing readings, I don't want to be your psychic forever. I want you to learn how to do this for yourself. The future is going to be filled with times of uncertainty. We are already experiencing that now. There is a lack of trust in our future, and fear fills many people's minds about their decisions. Having psychic abilities is going to shift how you navigate the future, and the most successful and influential people will be those who can use their psychic abilities to lead.

For many years, psychics have been a very taboo subject, and I know many people still feel uncomfortable because they don't understand the whole concept. I want to thank you for listening to my story, for trusting in what I share, and for keeping an open mind about how your life can change, too. My purpose is to activate you to the life you came here to live. If this resonates with you or you would like to venture even deeper into energetics, spirit guides, psychic gifts, healing, or anything business-related, I invite you to join me in my Psychic Community. It's the most comprehensive psychic membership you will find, with over $40K worth of resources to assist you in this soul journey for anyone on a deep inner path. I have helped thousands of people shift their lives and I look forward to having the honor of guiding you as well.

—————

Carrie Cardozo is a Master Psychic Leader, Master Healer, Energy Worker, Author, Podcast Host, and Creator of Soul Theory & #1 Psychic Development Community. Carrie works with experts, authorities, and leaders in their field to teach them how to open, connect, and activate their gifts and understand how to use them with power, integrity, and accuracy in their business. Carrie also coaches and consults in the entrepreneurial and business fields and has a connection to energy few will ever be able to possess. This connection allows her to deliver information that guides her clients to more success and greater impact. Her sessions are one of a kind and will leave you in a new vibration and stepping into your power. Her purpose is to tap you back into your truth and activate your gifts to the greatest level possible, allowing you to make the impact in this world you came here to make!

Want to learn how to call on the most powerful spirit team and how to use them to expand every area of your life?

Click here for the Spirit Team Masterclass
https://carriecardozo.kartra.com/page/spiritteam
—

Join Carrie's FREE Psychic Community, Psychic Elegance here
https://carriecardozo.kartra.com/page/freecommunity
—

Facebook
https://www.facebook.com/carrie.d.cardozo
—

Instagram
https://www.instagram.com/stories/carriecardozo/
—

LinkedIn
https://www.linkedin.com/in/carrie-cardozo/
—

TikTok
https://www.tiktok.com/@carriecardozo?_t=8p4XGO9y1Wh&_r=1

Walking Into the Darkness to Turn on the Light

A STORY OF LOVE AND MERCY

By Justina Lee Black

As a child of the '60s who lived in the suburbs of Detroit, my life consisted of playing outside with my friends and watching variety shows with my family after dinner. One evening, I saw somebody playing guitar and became so intrigued that I asked my mother if she would buy me one. When she came home with what became my prize treasure, the whole trajectory of my life changed.

Suddenly, my father said we were moving to the country. It was the most horrific moment of my childhood. I'll never forget the day my siblings and I sat in the back of my father's pick-up truck, waving goodbye to the group of children left behind. Tears ran down my cheeks as he slowly drove away.

At first, the solitude was deafening, but soon, I grew to love the country. I rode my bike through the fields, making trails to new places I explored. I eventually found peace in writing poems that turned into songs. I'd find the biggest, shady tree to strum my guitar under while the melodies echoed through the wind.

As a teen in the '70s, I had always stood out from the crowd. I towered over most boys, and my crystal blue eyes were the envy of the girls. I held a unique presence in both stature and spirit. Despite the world telling me I should try modeling, I found solace in being behind the camera. In high school, I enrolled in the yearbook class and became the class photographer. Along with journalism and creative writing classes, my life became a way to capture moments rather than being the subject of them. Writing became my sanctuary, where I could pour my thoughts and emotions onto paper, freeing my mind and soul.

I then began to write a diary, which was normal for a girl of 14 in 1974. But with me, it continued for decades. I felt like my life was special, and my story needed to be told. As the years passed, my diary became a chronicle of my life, documenting the joys and sorrows I experienced, a testament to my resilience and strength. For decades, my life was in those pages, and then a significant turn of events happened in my early 50s. It brought an unexpected challenge, and I had no choice but to concur. My life became like a double-edged sword; it was the best of times and the worst. I relied on faith, and my inner light guided me through the darkness.

Through it all, I never lost sight of who I was—a proud mother, a storyteller, a musician, a survivor. My life, though filled with twists and turns, was a good life. Then, one day, I received that fateful call. A voice introduced himself as the FBI, and when he proceeded to read me my rights, tears flowed uncontrollably. I was devastated and in shock. Suddenly, a five-year tax evasion battle consumed my life from simply signing three years of corporate tax returns.

My woman's intuition made me uncomfortable when my Certified Public Accountant of six years explained that two or three extensions were normal with corporate taxes, so not to worry. Starting a new business and not knowing corporate tax law, I trusted him because he was a friendly confidant, so I signed where the sticky pink arrow pointed.

During my first consultation with a prominent tax attorney, I asked why trusting my CPA was a crime, and why it wasn't his fault for misleading the IRS. He told me most people don't know tax law, but once you sign, the CPA is not liable. He witnessed my naive innocence and took an immediate liking to me. He told me he'd do everything he could to keep me from going to prison.

After five grueling years and a $50,000 legal lien on my Michigan home, he advised me to take a plea or go to trial.

My taxes were so confusing that the IRS still didn't know what I owed, but also knew too much time had gone by. The judge told us to go into the chamber and figure it out. We finally agreed I would pay back $100,000 in restitution and have 12 months of tethered house arrest. My lawyer was saddened and stunned when the judge added 30 days in the Miami Federal Penitentiary to make an example out of me. I sadly had to accept responsibility for a crime I did not commit, but I stood strong during my sentence with my husband looking on in disbelief. I was relieved that I was not sentenced to the Detroit Federal Prison System. Since Florida had become my legal home, The Federal Detention Center in Miami was an option I was able to take.

After 12 months of tethered house arrest, it was time to turn myself in. On June 16, 2016, my nightmare began. It was a dark turning point to my next 30 days as I walked into the walls of the unknown. Ironically, the prison had no record of me, so the process became a living hell.

Once the Marshals decided to process me, a stocky female prison guard broke the silence and abruptly opened the door and yelled, "Stand up!" She frisked me with her firm hands and efficiently fastened the cold metal shackles around my wrists. When she bent down to attach them to my ankles, she noticed my toe ring, a silver shooting star. It was a gift my husband bought at an art show that represented how I feel as an artist.

"Take it off!" she demanded. When I handed it to her, it was thrown in the garbage; the first part of breaking a prisoner's spirit was stripping them of everything they loved.

Once she was satisfied with her work of fastening my ankles, she opened the door and yelled, "Walk!" The weight of the iron dragged down on me as if trying to anchor me to the ground. I grimaced, regretting my choice of attire—the delicate black strappy sandals and patterned dress now felt absurdly out of place in this grim setting. I wanted to look nice for an upscale dinner by the ocean when Ken arrived upon my release, but there I was, shackled and helpless as the weight of the cold metal shackles dug into my ankles. Every step was painful. I struggled to keep moving forward.

The sound of clinking chains echoed through the narrow hallway, emphasizing my captivity as I walked down the hall of shame. I felt the weight of the male prisoners' stares as they lined up to be bussed to an undisclosed location. Their eyes followed my every move, their curiosity palpable. Unnerved by the intensity of their gazes, I quickened my pace, trying to shield myself from their scrutiny with the female guard close behind, pacing and rattling her keys. The stark, dimly lit tunnel felt suffocating, the blue door at the end like a beacon of hope in a sea of despair.

As we neared the door, a sense of foreboding gripped me. The arrival of another female guard, with her commanding presence, only heightened my unease. With a jingle of keys and a loudspeaker giving us passage, the metal door swung open, exposing a frigid cell that awaited me where three other female inmates sat in deep conversation, speaking Spanish. The guard then asked me to raise my arms and relieved me of my wrist shackles.

The chill of blowing frigid air seeped into my bones, contrasting sharply with the heat of anxiety that burned within me. When the door opened, a guard came and ushered the other inmates out, leaving me behind. It felt like hours had passed, and I was forgotten. I was freezing cold in my summer dress, so I walked back and forth to keep warm. Exhausted, I finally sat down on the cold white bench, sinking my head down to my knees. Seeing my shackles close up for the first time, I examined them and counted the links one by one. There were 29 links between my red, swollen ankles. As I focused under the bench, I saw the words *"God Saves"* carved into the wall, which made me smile. I then looked across the cell and read, *"Jesus loves you."* It gave me comfort that other Christians were also persecuted unjustly, so I prayed.

It felt like hours before the door opened. Weak and frozen to the bone, it was hard to get up to walk. I was ushered down a hallway to a different holding area, noticeably warmer and more welcoming; it was time for my mugshot. My mind began to race. My mugshot will go down in history. Do I smile, frown, or show anger or remorse? At the perfect moment, I chose a soft smile, then click, and it was done. Fingerprinting was next, then off to another holding cell where I was handed a sack lunch. The peanut butter and jelly sandwich tasted so good, and the red apple was a real treat.

When the door opened, I felt a strange and unsettling moment, only to be welcomed by the firm gaze of the new female guard in charge. She gathered a few other inmates and took us to the next area. It was time for a strip search. The click of the shackles being removed from our ankles one by one echoed in the air, signaling a shift in the energy of relief. None of the ladies dared to speak, the heavy silence hanging over us.

The guard demanded that we stand in one of the red circles painted on the ground and disrobe. Her eyes scanned each of us as we stood like mannequins with an empty stare. Her penetrating and suspicious stern voice asked us if we carried any contraband and, if we did, to turn it over now. When no one did, she demanded we turn around and bend over. The second thing they do in prison is stripping prisoners of their pride. With brisk efficiency, she began frisking us one by one.

After she completed her search, she took our clothes, handed each of us undergarments and a tan uniform, and said to get dressed. Her demeanor softened as she handed us clothing, which consisted of four pairs of huge white granny panties, four white T-shirts, two muumuu-style nightgowns, four towels, a washcloth, a hand towel, a set of sheets, and two more tan uniforms. She then asked our shoe size and handed us manly-looking black Crocs. The air crackled with tension, signaling the beginning of a new chapter in this surreal realm of confinement.

Dressed in our tan uniforms, we were then taken to an elevator with a kinder female guard who was much smaller than the rest and had flowing blonde hair. When the doors opened, we were told to get in and face the back wall. The third thing they do in prison is to make you feel vulnerable.

When we arrived at our destination, and the doors opened, we were told to turn around and file out one at a time and stand in line shoulder to shoulder. A group of guards were there chatting and laughing. They each welcomed the pretty blonde prison guard with a hug and kiss on her cheek. Her eyes then flickered with recognition as she exchanged greetings with the orderlies waiting for our arrival. They formed a peculiar camaraderie amidst the starkness of the facility's walls. It appeared to be a shift change. To the left, a huge metal door opened, welcoming in two female inmates dressed in green. I peered through the door before it slammed shut and got a glimpse of a bustling community of women in vibrant green, moving with purposeful energy.

The inmate next to me whispered, "That's the bad girls. The murderers, drug dealers, child abusers, and prostitutes."

When the blonde guard caught us gazing into the door, her stern voice interrupted our observations and demanded us to face forward. She then guided us toward a separate door to the right. As the huge metal door slowly opened, allowing us to file in, it offered a view of another group of women dressed uniformly in tan. Their presence created an air of anticipation as they eagerly queued up, waiting on an orderly who emptied two duffle bags of items on a table. She then began to sort them out with her helper, who called each inmate by name. As they approached, they were handed worldly treasures they ordered from the commissary and shuffled happily away.

I was relieved to see the area relatively clean and the room filled with excitement. The blonde guard passed me off to a male floor guard. He told me I'd have to wait until shift change was over, that he was leaving, and to stay put until the night guard arrived.

My tension became calm as I looked around the huge oval area. There were three floors, one above and one below. As the central area cleared out, the night guard arrived on duty.

He checked me in, then handed me off to Teresa, the floor orderly. She had a caring demeanor that contrasted sharply with the harsh walls of the prison. Teresa beckoned me to follow her down a dimly lit corridor that echoed with the sound of distant voices. We entered a small office where she unlocked a cabinet and began to carefully select toiletries. She put them in a bag and added two small yellow pads of paper and two tiny pencils before handing them to me.

She explained the process of commissary orders. I was to fill out an order form by Wednesday for delivery on Thursday, provided someone had put money in my account. Since it was Thursday, I had missed the cut-off date and would not receive anything until the week after next.

Disappointment followed as the guard approached us. In his stern voice, he commanded, "Follow me," and without hesitation, I complied.

We arrived at a cell where a woman sat on the lower bunk bed, her warm smile contrasting with the cold surroundings. "Hi, I'm Carly," she said with a friendly Spanish accent.

Before I could process the introduction, the guard interrupted, instructing me to put my belongings down and follow him. In a neighboring cell, the guard pointed to a meager mattress on a bed frame and said, "Pick it up and follow me." He then explained the shortage of pillows. Unable to fathom the idea of sleeping without one, I silently complied, picked up the mattress, and followed the guard back to Carly's cell.

Carly, in contrast, seemed well-prepared for life behind bars, showcasing a treasure trove of food items in a steel cabinet on the floor, next to an empty cabinet that belonged to me she pointed out. She noticed my sadness and told me not to worry, I was welcome to whatever I wanted in her cabinet. She then specifically explained that we needed to be standing up in our cells for the headcount at 4 p.m. and again at 10 p.m. before the lights shut off.

I threw my mattress up on the top bunk, made my bed, and used my sack of new belongings as my pillow. When I finally lay down, a beam of light suddenly flashed on me through a long, narrow window next to my bed. It was a light offering a beam of magnificence to the American flag waving in the wind. I was out of the darkness.

The morning came fast, and breakfast was disgusting enough to throw in the trash. I'm on a Keto diet anyway, I thought, so I went back to my cell and began to read the welcome brochure. To my utter delight, an unexpected glimmer of excitement blossomed within me when I saw the mention of something extraordinary—a guitar! The thought alone sent a surge of joy coursing through my veins, and without a moment's hesitation, I knew I had to get my hands on it.

Propelled forward with a newfound sense of purpose as I made my way to the guard's office. Ignoring the usual protocol, I boldly announced my quest, inquiring about the elusive guitar mentioned in the brochure.

To my surprise, the guard's face lit up as he confirmed its existence. With a reassuring nod, he directed his gaze toward a cluttered shelf filled with games, where the guitar appeared to be waiting patiently on the top shelf. He retrieved the instrument from its dormant state and handed it to me. I smiled as I saw the musical name Lucida in the soundhole.

With Lucida's melodic embrace, I found solace and purpose, a reminder that even in the darkest of moments, the harmony of life's symphony could still be heard. It didn't take long, amidst the shadows of confinement, for me to find liberation in the music that emerged from my soul.

One fateful night, I had a dream that would change my life forever. As I stood on a gleaming stage, bathed in the spotlight's glow, I sang the soulful words "*Love and Mercy*" to a panel of superstar judges. They sat mesmerized by my celestial voice and lyrics.

When the dream ended, the melody of "*Love and Mercy*" lingered in my mind, and I was awakened to find myself compelled to translate the song's lyrics onto my little yellow pad of paper. With the help of the illuminating soft light of the American flag, I began writing the lyrics to "*Love and Mercy*" just as I heard it in my dream. It was the first of ten songs I wrote during those fateful days.

As soon as the guard office opened, I checked Lucida out and played the first chords that came to mind and began to sing my song. As a mystical being of light, sound and vibration, the lyrics of "*Love and Mercy*" emerged into life in a burst of vibrant colors and melodies.

As the prison inmates began to hear my newfound musical gift, the Bible study ladies recognized the divine essence woven into my music. I was invited to lead the Bible study worship and perform at an event they had been planning for the "Bad Girls in Green."

When the day came, the huge metal door slowly opened. Several guards escorted dozens of inmates in green to the chairs we carefully set up for our audience. I noticed an inmate I befriended on the second floor with many other inmates in tan. She smiled down at me, offering a thumbs-up and a wink. As I gleamed across the prison, other inmates in tan quietly began to funnel out of their cells, waiting for the unexpected.

With courage and conviction, I took a deep breath and proceeded with Lucida to the stage. The room was never so quiet, all eyes on me. I gracefully began strumming the chords to "*Love and Mercy*" as a beacon of hope and transformation. In that moment, the power of music transcended boundaries. My voice sang a glorious message of love as I united hearts and souls in a symphony of redemption and grace.

As the final notes of the song faded away, the "Bad Girls in Green" rose to their feet. Their cheers filled the room with pure, unadulterated emotion, along with my fellow inmates in tan. The guards went on high alert as they jumped up and cheered but then became calm, allowing the joyous noise.

Overwhelmed by the outpouring of love and acceptance, Lucida and I joined the inmates in celebration walking through the sea of green, exchanging high fives as a symbol of unity and newfound hope.

We all became one in God's mercy on a fateful day in that prison. The music became the catalyst for transformation, paving the way for a future where love and mercy reigned supreme, guided by the mystical presence of Lucida.

Through the power of music, *Love and Mercy* took root in the hearts of those who had long been forgotten by society. The transformation was nothing short of miraculous, a beacon of hope in a place where darkness reigned supreme.

And so, as the final chords of my melody faded into the stillness of the night, a sense of peace settled over the prison, paving the way for a future where redemption was not just a distant dream but a tangible reality.

In life, we all have experiences and stories to tell. Documenting them offers a sense of hope that even a fragment of your legacy could make the world a better place. I'm grateful you took the time to hear just a part of my 30-day journey. If I reignited your soul to know you can preserve and pursue your life's mission, even when you don't know its direction, I'm thankful to have moved you.

Living your best life ever and holding steadfast to your convictions is powerful, and remember to never allow anyone to break your spirit, because that's your soul.

At 62 years young, I finally authored my first book. It's my powerful 30-day journal titled, *29 Links in 30 Days*. It paints a vivid picture of what I witnessed behind bars, offering readers an intimate glimpse into the raw reality of prison life through my experience and the stories inmates shared with me. I anticipate its release this winter.

In the winter of 2020, I showcased my first original Christmas song, simply titled,

"It's Finally Christmas," a song of joy which was much needed due to the sorrow of Covid 19. I then released six of my love songs in 2022 called *"There's Hope for Love."* You can easily find my songs on your favorite listening site, along with my newest track, *"Love and Mercy."* This track is a reflection of that moment in time when my heartfelt song blended with emotions and experiences that changed lives.

Take a moment and visit my website (see link below), where you will find a tapestry of photos and music videos, along with stories told through my songs, each a testament to a life lived fully and passionately.

I hope my journey of self-discovery and creativity touches your heart and inspires you to embrace your own story with courage and grace.

Thank you for being here at His perfect moment in time.

Peace and Love... and Mercy

Justina Lee Black

LOVE and MERCY

You are worthy. You are love. You came to me. You are love.
Everywhere around you, everyone you see.
We are one in spirit. We are all one in need.
Love and Mercy, Love and Mercy. Love and Mercy... Love, Love.
Open your eyes and call me. Open your hearts to love.
You are all powerful, all together, we are love
Can't you? Can't you? Can't you feel, feel the power of the Lord?
Stand up, Stand up and ask for Mercy and Love.
Love and Mercy. We are all the power of love.
Love and Mercy, be one with the creator above
Love and Mercy. We are all the power of love.
Love and Mercy, be one with the creator above.
Love and Mercy. Love and Mercy, Love and Mercy... Love.

Justina Lee Black was born in Detroit and raised as a young girl with a fiery passion for music that burned brighter than the city lights at night. Moving to the countryside as a young teen, her love for music grew. During those years, she found solace in the melodies that seeped through the radio waves in the 1970s. As her creativity flourished, her fingers danced on her guitar strings in the dimly lit basements of her friends' homes. Little did she know, her soulful voice held a power that could move mountains.

It was in the walls of the award-winning Chippewa Valley High School Choir that Justina's voice truly found its strength, nurtured by the expert guidance of her mentor, Ellen Bowen. As she honed her craft with the influence of local legend Maestro Benjamin Michael Caruso, they performed under the enigmatic name of *"Justina's Secret,"* which shaped her musical journey. Their partnership spanned eight years, birthing timeless songs and spiritual masterpieces like, *"Peaceful Place,"* a true story of a girlfriend's dream as her child entered heaven. Other songs so magically profound that they would bring audiences to tears through whispered stories of love, loss, and everything in between.

In 2006, Justina made her escape to the tranquil shores of the Florida Keys with her new and beloved husband, Captain Ken Black, where the salty breeze carried the promise of a new chapter. Yet, the recession of 2008 forced them to wander to the dazzling lights of Las Vegas, a city pulsating with energy and rhythm. There, amidst the vibrant local music scene, Justina crossed paths with a talented song-writer-producer and a fellow Detroiter, Michael Wilde, forming the soulful guitar duo *"Black and Wilde."* They mesmerized audiences with their harmonious melodies with a Beauty and the Beast appeal. When Pianist Virtuoso Damon Balser heard Justina's voice, he welcomed her into his top 40 trio, *"Merlot,"* which created a resonance of an ongoing musical dream for Justina. Still, the time had come to move on.

By 2011, the serene call of the Florida Keys beckoned her back, offering a peaceful haven to let her musical spirit soar, but her life journey took an unexpected turn to the unknown. As the wheel of fate turned once more, Justina found herself drawn back to her roots in

Detroit in the summer of 2015, where her journey had first begun. The trials of Hurricane Irma in 2017 brought her back to the idyllic shores of Islamorada, in the Florida Keys, where she performs and longs to weave her magical songs into Sync Music for films and TV.

Life is but a perfect dream, JLB~~~*

For more insights into my captivating story, visit
Justinaleeblack.com.

—

Immerse yourself in a remarkable tale of a spirited soul
who found redemption and creativity in the midst of adversity
https://www.reverbnation.com/justinaleeblack

—

Facebook
https://www.facebook.com/JustinaLeeBlackMusic
https://www.facebook.com/JustinasGenuineCreations
https://www.facebook.com/justinasvisions

—

Instagram
https://www.instagram.com/justinasworld21

—

LinkedIn
https://www.linkedin.com/in/goodhealthandmusic

—

Spotify
https://open.spotify.com/artist/2u1RAVjXvaU19OeSjhB9Cc

Transforming Pain into Power

HOW ADVERSITY SHAPED MY ENTREPRENEURIAL SPIRIT

By Kim Russo

Growing up as a young girl, I used to jokingly say that I suffered from "middle child syndrome." I had the best family, but I lived in a household with an older sister with special needs due to a learning disability and a younger brother who was not only the baby but was naturally given extra attention from my father, who coached his baseball teams. I always had this feeling of wanting to be seen and validated. I also had to entertain myself, so I turned to art and creativity. I always loved crafts and envisioned someday creating my own business centered around art and design. Being artsy came naturally to me; my father was artistic, and my mom's sister was a fashion designer in New York City. Acknowledging my divine gift for art, I would show my creations to my parents to gain the special attention and validation that I craved so much.

Unfortunately, this need for extra attention led to unhealthy future relationships.

Throughout high school, I experienced being popular in classroom settings but not in larger groups, like during the dreaded lunchtime. This desire to be liked by everyone set the tone for relationships where I constantly sought validation from others. I became a people-pleaser,

39

always paying attention to anyone who showed interest in me and with whom I wanted to associate.

I would've considered myself an introvert at this time. During middle school lunchtime, I would eat fast and then call my mother on the payphone every day so as not to have to sit there feeling uncomfortable and ostracized, like I didn't belong with any group.

In high school, college, and all through my twenties, I finally had a few good friends, but I often gravitated toward people who would take advantage of my kindness and people-pleasing tendencies when I entered college at The Fashion Institute of Technology in New York City. When I was 30, I thought I had met my Prince Charming, who would set me free from all the bad friendships and relationships, someone who gave and did not just take. It was like no other relationship in the beginning. I was treated in a way that made me feel like a princess. I was spoiled.

I lived in New York City throughout my college years and for most of my young career in the packaging design world. Part of that NYC lifestyle was going out all the time. I liked to party with friends. We would go to festivals and clubs, mostly hanging out in the VIP sections. I was in a well-known club in the VIP section the night I met my Prince Charming.

He swept me off my feet, and as my mother would say, he was the "ultimate wooer." For our first official date, he took me to Ibiza, Spain. He had met my family before this trip, as they were in town because of my grandmother's recent passing.

He began buying me Louis Vuitton bags and taking me to amazing restaurants. We traveled extensively and enjoyed VIP access in every club. It felt like a fairy tale, a world far removed from what I was used to. This lifestyle was entirely foreign to me, and I never imagined someone like him coming into my life, genuinely liking and caring for me. We were both in other relationships when we met, but mine wasn't serious. And from his stories, it was clear he was done with his.

I assumed he ended his relationship when he asked me to go to Ibiza with him. However, things began to change after we returned. Miscommunication and awkwardness around money led me to believe that our courtship had fizzled out. He offered to put money into my account since he knew I wasn't making much as a production designer at a packaging design agency. Though it was uncomfortable, I had come to rely on it. When I confronted him about this arrangement, he became angry and didn't speak to me for days.

One night, when I thought it was all over between us, he called me. He had gotten into a fight with his ex, claiming it was about me. He had (supposedly) planned to surprise me with a concert, and she reacted after finding the tickets. The situation had escalated to the point where the police were involved. He instructed me to go to his home, which I had never visited, and retrieve money from his gutter to bail him out of jail.

It felt almost surreal, like something out of a movie.

I'd never been to that part of Long Island. I scheduled a car service to take me to his house. I showed up at the house to grab the cash, only to find his ex, her family, and a police officer all in the house. I felt pretty stranded, lost, and confused. He called me using his one phone call while I was at the house. I went home because it was late, made my way back to Astoria, Queens, and was contacted by his friend, who I met up with at the precinct the next morning. After all that we had experienced in a short time, I felt I needed to help. The friend couldn't wait the entire time. So, here I am in the suburbs of Long Island, standing in the parking lot to bail him out. His ex ended up getting a restraining order and was squatting in his house, or so he said. At this point, I didn't know what to believe.

After he was released, we went to a nearby diner, where he told me he needed to stay with me. I had to wait at a 7-Eleven down the road from his house while the police escorted him to retrieve his belongings. Now I have this person I've known for a very short time moving into my small apartment.

So things accelerated quickly, and he moved in with me. I felt really bad for him because I knew he didn't have any family. He lost his mother; he had no siblings and no connection to his father. But shortly after he moved in with me, my apartment wasn't good enough for him. So we moved into what he claimed to be the "ivory towers." As a true narcissist, he made sure I knew how much better my life would be with him. We moved to Long Island City, overlooking Manhattan—the most beautiful apartment building, the most beautiful apartment with the most beautiful view. It was an absolute dream.

That's when things started to unravel.

Red flags started to appear that I had been blind to before. Shortly after we moved in, he doubled the agreed-upon rent that I was going to contribute, which he knew I couldn't make. That is when I started to sense he was not as financially well off as he led me to believe.

About six months into the relationship, I found out I was getting some inheritance from my grandmother, and he immediately guilted me into needing it before I even received it. This was after taking many other trips to Miami and for Christmas that first year. We flew from Paris, first class, to Las Vegas to get VIP service for New Year's Eve. I fell ill that night, but he couldn't care less and proceeded to go out without me.

Because of all the trips and things we had done, he racked up an enormous credit card bill that had to be paid off or it was going into collections. Unbeknownst to me, the money he was spending was all a lie. By this time, I was in too deep. I was living with him. I had been recently laid off from the packaging design agency. They lost a big client, which forced layoffs, and I was part of the cut. I had already started helping him in his print shop, so naturally, I started working with him full-time.

There was so much office politics when I worked in the corporate packaging design environment, and now working in his business—I had no desire to be part of that. I've always dreamed of starting my own business, but self-doubt had me thinking I needed a business partner to do the "businessy" things. I never felt smart enough. Working in corporate for over ten years, I knew I wanted more creative control and autonomy over my life.

I thought this was a great opportunity, given the fact that he had a print shop and an apparently successful business—I was wrong.

This marked a pivotal moment where I believed we would have a great life together, building a business side by side. However, numerous challenging situations along the way made me begin to realize that I was fully capable of doing this on my own.

At the same time we decided to work together, the other print shop he was leasing from decided to close its business. His rent at the time was $1,000 so he had a few options. They were: find a new location, find a new tenant to share with, or take over the whole warehouse. Despite my caution, he decided to take the whole space, which was $7,000-$8,000 a month.

We had big goals and felt the pressure to produce enough money to cover the high rent for both our home and business. Whenever I offered advice, it was either ignored or later adopted as his idea, usually too late. He would accuse me of unintentionally emasculating him with my good ideas. Our "fancy lifestyle" came to a screeching halt, and tensions rose. Anything that went wrong was always blamed on me. We even joked that I had a pack of calculators on an auto-ship from Amazon because he would throw so many in my direction and break them when he was angry.

We were spending way too much time together. He had very few friends; the ones he had were much younger and were only his friends because he paid for VIP and bottle service. When that lifestyle faded, so did the "friends." He never liked my friends for some unknown reason; I believe he felt threatened. He always had to be "the best" in the room, which resulted in me losing touch along the way, living in seclusion, and letting my physical health go.

This is when the romance really started to die. It became more of a roommate/working relationship. We didn't travel anymore. We didn't socialize. We fought a lot—rather he fought at me—and he was constantly asking me for money. The only money I had at this point was my 401(k) from my corporate job. He didn't pay me to work with him; he just paid for us to live and mostly used my credit cards. This also resulted in him constantly badgering me that he paid for everything, completely discrediting any work I did to help grow the business close to seven figures. He eventually bullied me into pulling from my 401(k) because he didn't know how to run his business properly.

Everything was done to please him and keep him from flipping out; at this point, I was constantly walking on eggshells. Happiness was off the table—the goal was to make it through the day without an outburst. When I'd say I wanted to go out on the weekends, he'd take me to the office to work. There was no balance at all. This continued for three of the five years of our relationship as I held on to the brief life we had when we first met.

I knew it was over when we went on a trip to see my parents in Hilton Head for Thanksgiving. We visited with them for more than a week and then headed to Myrtle Beach for him to compete in an overly-priced toy car race. He had been complaining about having nothing fun to do, so I encouraged him to pick up his expensive childhood hobby of racing toy cars. He had to have the best, and when he lost races, guess whose fault it was? Mine!

When we were with my parents, he was very rude to my father on the first day, taking a conversation out of context and bringing it to an extreme, like he was self-sabotaging. That whole week, instead of spending time with my parents, I worked remotely on his business while he sat around and did nothing. After four years, it was the first time my father realized he was not a good person. I confided in my mother every single day, but I knew my dad, a strong Italian man, wouldn't handle it well if he knew what was really going on with his baby girl. I kept it from him as long as I could.

The week became incredibly uncomfortable once he started being rude to my father. I knew it was the beginning of the end. He would hide and be disrespectful, prompting my father to tell me it was time to leave the relationship. My dad set up an action plan for me to move out and live at my brother's. The plan started coming together, and I realized things would never improve. As soon as we pulled out of my parents' driveway, he immediately started screaming at me.

I was holding on to this dream that wasn't going to actually come back to reality. I started conceptualizing a plan. On Christmas of that year, my dog Zoe—my best friend for 14 years—got sick. We were home, just the two of us, and he was cooking when she began to have a seizure and scared me to death. We took her straight to the animal hospital. He paid $5,000 in medical bills right there on the spot, something I could not do since he controlled the finances.

That delayed the plan. Zoe became the focus and, in a strange way, brought us temporarily closer. I wouldn't let her leave my side, so she came to the office with us every day. It took me eight months after this to finally leave. Much longer than I intended.

I was also scared because I had no money, and he wasn't paying me. I had a lot of credit card debt that he had acquired. I felt very stuck because Zoe needed monthly medication, and I didn't have any way to pay off this debt. In the last month or so, I noticed he started to be a little bit nicer. He began to pay off my credit card bills, which I was relieved about. I was still so stressed about the relationship and Zoe being sick. He started traveling to the toy car races without me and left me to do all the work. I became so overworked, tired, and stressed.

During one of his trips, I visited my sister and nieces, three hours away. I didn't have a car since I depended heavily on him. I also got to the point where I was so removed from being independent that I didn't even know how to travel by myself anymore. He arranged for our driver, who we often hired, to drive me round trip. When I got to my sister's, I messaged him to tell him I got there safely, but I never heard back from him. He was very distant and detached, not even bothering to say hi to my nieces, which was unlike him.

While I was at my sister's the first night, Zoe had a few seizures, vomited, and fell down a flight of stairs. I thought she was surely gone, but she bounced back up—my nerves were shot. I went back to bed and, all of a sudden, had these crazy dizzy spells. For the next few months, I was constantly dizzy. I felt like the ground was moving all the time, and I was walking like I was on a boat. This was very uncomfortable. I consulted multiple doctors to figure out what was happening, but none of them had an answer. One night, he told me to relax because I was dizzy and wasn't feeling well. He gave me medication to help me sleep. Shortly after he left, I called to ask him a question, but he didn't answer his phone for hours until he returned home. I knew in my gut something was off. It just accelerated the dizziness and tension between the two of us.

He lied about where he was going and then did it again a few more times. I knew something was up. I finally confronted him at 6:30 in the morning and gave my 2-week notice.

He started to date, and because he still needed me to help run his business, I was able to use that as leverage during these two weeks to pay everything off that he owed me and have him pay to fly my childhood friend in. I rented a car, and he paid for the hotels to help me move to my brother's in Texas.

This is the moment On Brand Designs, Inc. was formed. A creative agency specializing in brand strategy, logo design, packaging design, marketing materials, and web design. My dream was starting to become a reality.

Yet I am grateful for this relationship for one reason: This experience taught me what I *didn't* want in a partner and how *not* to run a business. It gave me the confidence to realize that I didn't need a business partner; I could create a successful business on my own. However, he self-servingly helped me set up the business with his accountant, ensuring I could continue working for him since he couldn't run it without me. This also allowed him to avoid paying employee taxes.

We agreed on a monthly fee for me to help his business while growing mine. I was still feeling the loss of a five-year relationship, even though it had been soul-sucking. I had to work through the dependency. I call it the "limbo phase" when I tried to rebuild myself and build my business.

THE BEST THING I EVER DID WAS WORK ON MYSELF!

I got back into fitness as I had let myself go physically, mentally—everything. Shortly after moving in with my brother and his wife outside of Dallas, we all relocated to the suburbs of Illinois for his job. I hate to admit it, but although I was super grateful to have the support, I was a little dissatisfied about moving back to the cold.

When I started to date again, I realized I was still attracting the wrong men. I could see my people-pleasing tendencies creep back in, and I would date for the wrong reasons.

The big shift came when I hired a relationship coach! Back to working on myself, I was ready to be on my own, and I knew my brother and sister-in-law were ready, too.

I knew one thing for sure: I wanted warm weather, sunshine, and a coastal environment to focus on growing my design business. I chose Charleston, South Carolina.

It was close to my parents but not *too* close. This was a bold move for me. I didn't know anyone in Charleston and had only been there twice for a few hours. So, I packed up my stuff and stayed with my parents while I set up my place in Charleston with Zoe. As soon as I was ready to move into my apartment, Zoe passed away. She was there for me through the year of healing, and I didn't know if I could get through the move without her.

In January 2020, I moved into my apartment in Charleston. I took time working with the relationship coach to help with accountability, grow my business, and make friends before I could even think about dating.

Once I had made a few friends, I was ready. With the guidance of a relationship coach, I went on a few dates for a couple of weeks, and I met my current partner through networking in February 2020. I knew after the first weekend together that I had found the one.

A couple of weeks into our relationship, the COVID lockdown happened, and we quarantined together at his condo in Myrtle Beach to have private beach access when most couldn't. He couldn't rent it out due to the COVID restrictions. I was really grateful that all my intentions for making friends and a partner manifested when they did.

During the early months of lockdown, work was slow. I knew I wanted more. During this time, we were traveling back and forth from Charleston to Myrtle Beach, and I would have the same conversation on repeat about wanting better.

I was still very dependent on my ex's business to support myself. I was focusing on how to break free from this person altogether and how to grow my business. I was working in this freelancer mindset, taking any design project that came my way, even if it wasn't really something I wanted to do. I knew I wanted a team. I knew I wanted more of an agency. I just felt stuck because I didn't know how to achieve this.

I wanted to do work that drove me and ignited my passion for my craft. I also wanted to make more money, and I knew I had to shift my business to make that happen.

I remembered how much the relationship coach helped me, so I invested by hiring coaches and consultants. I took courses and began networking. This was a game-changer. The advice from a few coaches helped me set up systems and hire a team. While still working with my ex, I built my team with the full support and understanding of my dream man, which made the process much easier.

Once I hired a team, I began working less for my ex because I focused more on my own business. I knew I had to keep pushing to build a six-figure business without his contribution, and that's exactly what I did. It took four out of my six years in business to part ways with him. It felt like the biggest accomplishment. I knew I could do this when I created a six-figure business on my own.

The confidence and shifts in my mindset and business have inspired me to achieve and create things I never thought possible. I was inspired to take all that I invested in my designs and branding business and create a course and a coaching business for other creatives to teach what worked and eliminate what didn't. It's brought a newfound passion to take my people-pleasing ways and use them for good to help others in a more impactful and positive way that is not harmful to myself. The course is designed for creatives looking to go from freelancer to business owner, just like me.

Something I would've never imagined is being able to use my voice to reach others. I now consider myself an introvert turned extrovert. I never thought I could be on a podcast, let alone host a podcast called *The Profitable Brand Designer*. This time was really about working on myself, working on my business, becoming visible, and growing more confident, all while being truly admired and loved by my person.

I love my business because it allows me to design for clients and create impactful brands using my intuitive design skills. I am passionate about what I do and find joy in the design process.

My relationship is now going into its fifth year and is in sharp contrast to my past. I've worked so much on my mindset and manifesting. I credit him for building my confidence and newfound extroverted personality because he is so personable and loves people, something I was not accustomed to in past relationships.

He is incredibly supportive and never feels threatened by my big ideas. He allows me to be my authentic self and embrace my high-achiever, alpha-femme ways.

So, after being together for three years (and after learning not to move in with somebody so quickly), we moved in together. I learned a lesson from my previous relationships: I need to have my own space. I came up with an idea to put a "she-shed" in the backyard to have my own place for myself and my business. It's my place, it's my safe space, it's my creative space, and it's a healthy space.

My "she-shed" has become well-known in the Charleston area with local female entrepreneurs. I've also had the great fortune of being featured in a local magazine, showing off my unique creative space.

I consider myself very fortunate to have the unwavering support of my partner. Knowing I prefer to eat healthy but dislike cooking, he prepares all my meals and brings them to me in my "she-shed," allowing me to focus on creating the brand and business I love. He also supports the healthy lifestyle I desire by ensuring we stay active and go to the gym every morning. In our four years together, we've had very few disagreements and always find a way to resolve any challenges we face. We prefer spending our time filled with love and laughter, not arguments.

We like to listen to self-development books and interpret the philosophies together. We like to work on manifestations together and discuss our long-term goals. We launched *The Profitable Brand Designer* podcast together to help educate others on business, entrepreneurship as a couple, and how to maintain a healthy, balanced mindset.

In our first episode, I discuss how I manifested both my happy relationship and thriving business. I reveal the key actions that led to my transformation and share how I applied the same techniques used to manifest my partner to build my business.

How did I manifest the future that I wanted? When I was first working with the relationship coach, I had an exercise where I had to put together a list of all the things I wanted in a partner. Without even realizing it, that list ended up being all the things I didn't want from all my exes and all my bad relationships.

My coach had me take this list and turn it into a positive. That was another couple of weeks of contemplation. Then, I took the list and put it in order of priority. The order shifted when I started to realize: *Do I really want somebody like this if they're not [X]?* I did that same practice for my business. *What do I want in my business? What do I want from my clients? What are the big goals that I have for the business?* I do come back to this exercise once in a while to make sure that I am visualizing the path I want and working toward those goals. I'd love to share this practice with you: Manifest Your Dream Partner + Business.

Some lessons I've learned from my journey are that trusting in yourself and being confident are crucial steps in growing a healthy relationship and a profitable business. A positive mindset, goal-setting, and continuous self-development are key components. During this time of healing and self-improvement, I've started networking and surrounding myself with supportive people who share similar goals. I stay committed to the actual work and never give up. One of the most impactful routines I've adopted is practicing gratitude *every day*, something I had never done before.

And I'm grateful and thankful for all the things that I have done. I'm grateful for the people I've been able to help and those who have helped me. I'm grateful for all the comforts that I have and the ability to create my life.

Kim Russo is the CEO, Lead Brand + Graphic Designer, VIP Brand Strategist, and Creator of "The Profitable Brand Designer" Course, which teaches creatives how to switch their mindset from freelancer to entrepreneur and create a profitable design business.

She also stands as the visionary force behind On Brand Designs, an exclusive design studio in Charleston, SC's vibrant heart. As the Founder, CEO, and Lead Designer, she not only shapes visual experiences but also empowers her clients and team.

Kim began her career working for top packaging design agencies in NYC after getting her degree from the Fashion Institute of Technology. In 2018, after spending her entire career in corporate, Kim decided she was ready to make a bigger impact on a smaller scale. She left the "Big Apple" and started On Brand Designs, which launched in September 2018. Kim moved to Charleston in 2020 and has been focused on growing her business ever since.

Her areas of expertise include brand strategy, brand identity, website design, print graphics, and packaging design. She loves creating scroll-stopping designs for female entrepreneurs that make you say, "Ooo, I love that!" When she is not busy working, Kim enjoys crafting, painting pet portraits, and lying on the beach or by the pool with her friends and family.

For more information or to contact Kim
https://on-brand-designs.myflodesk.com/manifest-love-business
—
And listen to her podcast here
https://podcasts.apple.com/us/podcast/the-profitable-brand-designer/
id1748594999
—
Website
https://onbranddesigns.com
—
Facebook
https://www.facebook.com/kimberly.russo.334/
—
Instagram
https://www.instagram.com/on_brand_designs/
—
TikTok
https://www.tiktok.com/@onbranddesigns
—
LinkedIn
https://www.linkedin.com/in/kimberly-russo/
—
Pinterest
https://www.pinterest.com/onbranddesigns/_created/
—
Etsy
https://www.etsy.com/shop/aSpotOfPaintByKim
—
YouTube
https://www.youtube.com/@onbranddesigns

Unpaved Path to Greatness

BECOMING WHO YOU ARE MEANT TO BE

By Klara Nemes Brown

Since I started my career as a therapist, I always had a deep desire and passion for solving relationship challenges, especially working with women. My appreciation and love for women developed from my own pain, and I believed for a long time that being a woman put us in a position of having less privilege in life. I believe relating to another human being, especially in a romantic relationship, is the hardest task we're ever going to have to deal with. In this chapter, my intention is to demonstrate that we, as women, have the power to create and build a wide range of deep connections that can bring healing on a personal level but also to the world. My deep desire is to impact countless women's lives who are living alone because they are afraid of being hurt again or don't think they deserve to be loved. And it starts with healing oneself, then reclaiming your power and choosing your own destiny. I want to share tools and exercises for building a conscious partnership, drawing on both personal and professional experiences that include challenges, mistakes, failures, and transformative lessons from my own life.

I came to believe that no matter how grim circumstances might seem, one always has the power to reshape their destiny. This recognition didn't come by learning from books but by walking on the uncharted path and having a strong commitment to never give up until I become the woman I was born to be and step into my highest potential. Today, I am running a successful business as a coach. I have been married for 23 years to a man who is the love of my life. He has matched me on every level, and each morning, I wake up with deep-rooted gratitude that, by the grace of God, I live a life that I absolutely love. But my life wasn't always like that.

I was born and raised in Hungary. My parents were not the role models I needed to learn how to relate to others. They were the byproduct of World War II, poverty, and dysfunctional family origins. They never learned or heard about emotional intelligence that might help them relate to each other. There was a lot of screaming, yelling, and flying dishes in our home. I was an only child and grew up without feeling loved or belonging in my family. My mother was disappointed because she wanted a boy. I think deep down, she believed boys have more privilege and an easier life than women. I was a rebellious child with a strong will. My escape from the family drama at night was in reading fairy tales and dreaming that when I grew up, I would be able to conquer all the obstacles, just like my heroes, and reach the stars. By age 27, I was a single mom. I came to the States as a refugee with two suitcases to overcome the shadows of my early traumas. I didn't speak any English, but I wanted to build a new life and new relationships. My driving force—besides my deep love for my daughter—was a strong conviction in myself that I was meant for more. My story is not different than most women's. Many women experience broken hearts at some point in their lives and are disappointed by men... maybe more than once. After two divorces, the last at age 34, I wondered how two men with such different characteristics—one was an alcoholic who wrecked our lives, and the other was kind, attentive, and loving—both ended up with divorce.

All my life, I looked for love, care, and validation from powerful men who made me feel good about myself. I was an independent, hardworking woman who was successful in my career. But inside, I was lonely and unhappy. I struggled with what was wrong with me and blamed myself for relationships that didn't work.

After my second marriage ended, I fell into a dark place. I felt a sense of emptiness and loneliness and was scared of what the future would bring. I slipped into a major depression. My daughter kept me from giving up. One morning, I looked into the mirror and told myself I was *meant for more,* and I promised myself that I would find a way. This experience changed my life forever. This declaration sent me on a 15-year journey to find a better way. On this quest, I dug deep and began to really know myself. I regained confidence and developed tools and strategies that I learned from the best mentors. Finally, I moved from healing to transforming my life. I broke my cycle of failed relationships. Now, instead of feeling empty, I feel confident and whole. Instead of feeling lonely and scared, I feel free and in charge of my life.

In the last two decades—working as a therapist and getting my certification as a woman-centered transformational coach—I have helped thousands of women achieve confidence and feel free to take charge of making their dream relationship a reality.

Now, I will introduce you to three steps of my coaching program: creating your destiny vision, breaking free from limiting beliefs, and understanding the compatibility that propels you to step into your empowered future. This is where you start to design a successful relationship and the life you deserve. I developed my coaching program with 20 years of learning, practicing, and implementing my strategies to prove its validity. I want to acknowledge Dr. Claire Zammit, my mentor, who trained me in the woman-centered transformational program and contributed to my coaching program with her feminine power principles.

CREATE YOUR DESTINY VISION

A destiny vision is not a construct borne from feelings of inadequacy or external pressures; it transcends superficial needs and societal expectations. It originates from our innermost selves, reflecting a profound yearning to manifest our highest aspirations. This vision embodies our deepest desires for love, connection, and the ability to give and receive freely. Ultimately, it is an expression of our potential to live fully and authentically, aligned with the highest possibilities of our existence.

In every journey, the destination must be clear before the path can be determined. Relationships, especially romantic ones, are no different. A relationship without a clear vision is like a ship without a compass: adrift, susceptible to the whims of external forces, and likely to end up somewhere unintended. As we embark on the journey to designing your dream relationship, the first and most crucial step is to understand the power of having a vision.

From a young age, many of us are influenced by fairy tales, movies, and societal expectations, leading us to form vague ideas of what love and relationships should look like. These ideas are often shaped by external factors rather than our true desires and needs. When we enter relationships without a clear vision, we rely on these external influences, which can result in repeated patterns of dissatisfaction and unfulfillment.

A clear vision is essential because it acts as a guiding star, helping you navigate the complexities of love with purpose and direction. It enables you to recognize what you truly desire in a partner and a relationship, making it easier to make decisions that align with your goals. When your vision is clear, you can communicate your needs effectively, setting the foundation for a relationship that supports your growth and well-being.

However, creating a vision for your relationship is not just about listing desired traits in a partner or imagining the perfect date. It's a deeper, more introspective process that involves understanding your core values, reflecting on past experiences, and identifying what truly matters to you. This vision must be aligned with who you are at your core, not just what you think you should want. To create your vision, it is crucial to understand your deepest desires, needs, and wants from a relationship. You may be yearning to attract and create a growth-oriented relationship where you are "met" on all levels: emotional, mental, physical, and spiritual. You don't just come together in some form of partnership or marriage to raise a family and create security but also for support to self-actualize. You should be loved unconditionally for who you are and be fiercely supported to become the best version of yourself.

As a relationship coach, I've seen countless women transform their love lives simply by getting clear on their vision. Women who once felt lost or trapped in unsatisfying relationships found new purpose and direction by defining what they wanted in a relationship and who they wanted to be in that relationship. The process of creating a vision not only empowers you to attract the right partner but also helps you become the woman you were meant to be.

One common mistake women make, especially after a painful breakup or divorce, is rushing into a new relationship without taking the time to clarify their vision. This often leads to repeating the same patterns, choosing partners who don't align with their values, and ultimately feeling unfulfilled. The first step to breaking this cycle is to pause, reflect, and create a vision that truly resonates with your deepest desires.

Creating a vision for your relationship begins with introspection. It's about asking yourself the right questions: *What do I truly desire in a partner? What values are non-negotiable for me? How do I want to feel in my relationship? What kind of life do I want to build with my partner?* These questions help you gain clarity on what's most important to you, allowing you to focus on building a relationship that aligns with your true self.

Before we continue, let me introduce an exercise to anchor your destiny intention.

I invite you to put everything aside, and we'll begin our practice of shifting our attention from ordinary awareness to extraordinary awareness. If you feel comfortable, close your eyes and allow your awareness to drop down into your body, all the way down into your hips, down into your legs, down into the soles of your feet, and into the earth.

With each breath, take your attention away from all the places where it may have been so far today and bring 100 percent of your attention back inside your own body. Connecting with these deeper, most powerful parts of you—places where you show up as a friend or in your work, or when you are expressing your creativity—is where you feel most yourself. Letting your awareness deepen and soften, let go of control and the need to know answers to any questions of your life: the who, the how, the when. As you connect to your most powerful self, ask these questions: *What kind of relationship do I desire? How do I want to feel, experience, express, and create in this area of my life?* Then, wait for the answers. After writing them down, create a power statement that sounds like this:

"I attract an authentic, meaningful relationship where love and trust are abundant, and where I am free to express my love fully, and I am supported in becoming the woman I was meant to be."

After creating your vision, visualize the kind of partnership that will bring you lasting happiness. This process is about more than just finding a partner. It's about designing a relationship that aligns with who you are and what you want out of life. This empowering process requires deep reflection and intentionality. It's about envisioning the life you want to build with a partner and understanding the qualities and values that are essential for that relationship to thrive.

Visualization is a powerful tool that helps you mentally create the relationship you desire before it manifests in your life. To begin this process, find a quiet space where you can relax and let your imagination flow.

Close your eyes and imagine your ideal relationship. Think about the qualities your partner possesses, how you interact with each other, and the life you want to build together. Visualize the day-to-day experiences—how you communicate, support each other's dreams, and handle challenges. Imagine the emotions you feel in this relationship—love, trust, respect, and joy.

As you visualize, be specific. Consider details like how you spend your time together, the kinds of activities you enjoy, and how you support each other's personal growth. The more detailed your vision, the clearer your path will become.

Once you've created a detailed vision in your mind, it's important to write it down and keep it within reach so that you can refer to it regularly. This document is your blueprint for building the relationship of your dreams.

Finally, remember that creating a vision is not a one-time task. As you grow and evolve, your vision may change, and that's perfectly okay. The key is to stay aligned with your core values and desires, adjusting your vision as needed to reflect your personal growth and changing circumstances.

You have a desire, and you have your vision; you're now prepared to embark on the next step of your journey. There are barriers that may be holding you back from realizing your vision. Transformation has to happen.

DISCOVER YOUR BARRIERS

As you continue your journey toward creating your dream relationship, it's essential to address those significant obstacles that can hinder your progress: shame-based beliefs. These beliefs are often deeply ingrained and shaped by past experiences, societal conditioning, or repeated patterns of behavior. They act as invisible barriers that exist on the level of identity, so problematic because what happens is that they are shaping our perception, our interpretations, and our choices, and how we are responding in ways that are incredibly far-reaching. They are holding you back from fully embracing the love and happiness you deserve. Breaking free from these shame-based beliefs is a crucial step in cultivating your authentic self and building the relationship of your dreams.

IDENTIFY YOUR SHAME-BASED BELIEFS

Here are some questions to help you uncover and disrupt your shame-based beliefs:

- What negative thoughts do I have about myself or my ability to form relationships?
- What patterns do I notice in my relationships that might be linked to these beliefs?
- What fears do I have about love, commitment, or being vulnerable?

The first step in breaking free from shame-based beliefs is to identify them. This requires honest self-reflection and a willingness to explore the thoughts and patterns that have been holding you back. Let me guide you through an exercise to discover your core beliefs regarding your relationship challenges.

Please sit comfortably and close your eyes if you wish. Let's take a couple of deep breaths. With every breath you take, let your awareness deepen into your body, into your hips, your legs, and into the earth. See if you can step into the part of yourself where you feel your most authentic self. It might be when you're walking in the woods, at work, or the place where you feel most creative. Connect with that part of yourself and bring her fully here.

From this place of connection to a deeper source of love and wisdom, this mature and wise woman that you are, I want to invite you to reflect upon the following:

- What have been the challenges or struggles that you have had in this area of your life up until now?
- It's very important to separate how you feel about each area of your life and think about what actually happened that caused you to stop or become stuck. What happens when you get stuck or stopped?
- What are the patterns that keep repeating themselves?
- What feedback do you get back from others over and over again?
- What do you sense is the root of the issue for you?

These questions help you get your core beliefs about yourself, others, and life. Let's consider a possible pattern.

You might become emotionally invested in a new relationship and then find out the person is unavailable or doesn't want to commit. This might happen again and again in different situations. It could be a pattern with every person you've ever been in a relationship with. You may have thoughts like these:

- I don't matter. I am not loveable. I am a failure.
- Men don't want to commit, are unavailable, or only want younger women.

- I'll never find true love; all my relationships end with failure.

As you reflect on these questions and thoughts, you may start to see recurring themes. Perhaps you've noticed that you often sabotage relationships when they start to get serious, or you consistently attract partners who are emotionally unavailable. These patterns can be clues to the underlying beliefs that are influencing your behavior.

It's important to recognize that shame-based beliefs are not truths; they are rooted in a part of yourself where you are disconnected from your power. In my coaching program, I will take you through various exercises to make these barriers visible, interrupt them, and break through them in a very powerful and direct way. So you can open yourself up to new possibilities and create a life that aligns with your true desires.

RECLAIM YOUR POWER AND CULTIVATE YOUR AUTHENTIC SELF

As you begin the process and are able to reclaim your power, you are taking an important step toward cultivating your authentic self. Your authentic self is the person you are when you are true to your values, desires, and potential and are free from the constraints of fear and doubt.

As you release these beliefs and embrace your authentic self, you will find that you approach relationships with greater confidence, clarity, and purpose. You will no longer be held back by fear or doubt, but instead, you will be empowered to create the relationship you've always dreamed of. Breaking free from shame-based beliefs is a powerful and transformative process.

BREAKING FREE FROM SHAMED-BASED BELIEFS

As you begin to break free from barriers, you will find that your confidence and sense of self-worth start to grow. This newfound strength empowers you to approach relationships with a clearer understanding of what you truly want and deserve. However, this process is ongoing and requires consistent effort to maintain your new beliefs and new identity.

To ensure that these new, empowering beliefs take root, it's essential to reinforce them consistently. Here are some strategies and resources to help you solidify your new growth mindset.

- Morning Mindfulness Practice
- Self-reflection—Journal
- Meditate
- Gratitude—Write down three things you are grateful for
- Visualize
- Daily affirmation practice
- Surround yourself with like-minded women

With each step you take towards releasing the past and embracing your true self, you move closer to the relationship and life you've always dreamed of.

In this new reality, you are no longer searching for someone "out there" to complete you or fulfill your needs. Instead, you recognize that you have the power to create and define your own destiny. You understand that a healthy, fulfilling relationship is not about finding someone who meets a checklist of criteria but about building a partnership based on mutual respect, love, and growth.

EMPOWERMENT THROUGH TRANSFORMATION

Transformation is not just about healing the past—it's about empowering yourself to create a future that aligns with your highest potential. You are no longer defined by your past experiences but by the choices you make in the present and the vision you hold for the future.

With your new identity and clear vision, you'll be ready to take the steps necessary to attract and build the relationship that will bring you lasting joy and fulfillment. We now turn our focus to a critical element in the foundation of lasting love: compatibility.

UNDERSTANDING COMPATIBILITY

Compatibility is the cornerstone of lasting love. It's what allows you and your partner to build a relationship that is not only strong and resilient but also deeply fulfilling. By focusing on shared values, aligned goals, emotional connection, effective communication, and healthy conflict-resolution skills, you create a partnership that can withstand the test of time.

Compatibility is not merely about liking the same things or having similar interests; it's about aligning on deeper levels, such as values, life goals, emotional needs, and communication styles. When two people are truly compatible, they can create a relationship that is resilient, fulfilling, and capable of withstanding the test of time.

THE IMPORTANCE OF COMPATIBILITY IN RELATIONSHIPS

Compatibility plays a vital role in the success of any relationship. It influences how well partners connect with each other, how they handle challenges, and how satisfied they are in their partnership. Without compatibility, even the strongest attraction or initial chemistry can fade, leading to misunderstandings, conflicts, and, ultimately, a breakdown in the relationship.

Compatibility is about more than just getting along—it's about creating a partnership where both individuals feel understood, valued, and supported. It's the foundation upon which a healthy, lasting relationship is built.

KEY TRAITS OF COMPATIBILITY

Compatibility is multifaceted, encompassing various aspects of your relationship that contribute to harmony and mutual understanding. These traits are the building blocks of a strong and enduring connection. Here are the key traits of compatibility to focus on:

1. **Shared core values.** At the heart of compatibility are shared core values. These are the fundamental beliefs and principles that guide your life decisions and behavior. When you and your partner share core values, you create a solid foundation for mutual respect, trust, and understanding. Examples of core values are honesty, integrity, commitment to family, spiritual beliefs, work ethic, and personal growth.

2. **Emotional intelligence.** Emotional intelligence (EQ) is the ability to recognize, understand, and manage your own emotions, as well as those of others. High emotional intelligence is crucial for compatibility, as it enables you to navigate the emotional landscape of your relationship with empathy and understanding. Traits of high EQ: self-awareness, empathy, emotional regulation, and effective communication.

3. **Aligned life goals.** Aligned life goals are essential for long-term compatibility. These goals include your aspirations for the future, such as career ambitions, family planning, financial stability, and lifestyle preferences. When you and your partner share similar goals, you're more likely to work together towards a common vision for your life. Examples of life goals are starting a family, building a successful career, traveling the world, or pursuing personal development.

4. **Communication style.** Effective communication is key to maintaining compatibility. Understanding and respecting each other's communication styles can prevent misunderstandings and foster a more harmonious relationship. Communication style examples: direct and assertive, empathetic and supportive, or reserved and reflective.

5. **Conflict resolution approach.** How you and your partner handle conflicts is a strong indicator of compatibility. A compatible conflict resolution approach involves working together to find solutions that meet both partners' needs without damaging the relationship. Healthy conflict resolution traits include a willingness to compromise, focus

on solutions rather than blame, and stay calm under pressure.

6. **Mutual respect.** Mutual respect is the foundation of any healthy relationship. It involves valuing each other's opinions, boundaries, and individuality. Respecting your partner as an equal and appreciating their unique qualities is crucial for maintaining compatibility. Examples of mutual respect are supporting each other's goals, respecting boundaries, and appreciating differences.

When you find a partner with whom you are truly compatible, the relationship that unfolds is rich in meaning and purpose. It is not merely about enjoying each other's company or having shared interests —although those are important—but about connecting on a deeper level where your values, goals, and emotional needs are fully aligned. This kind of relationship supports your growth, encourages your aspirations, and helps you navigate life's challenges with a sense of unity and purpose.

In a relationship rooted in compatibility:

- You feel understood.
- You are supported in your growth.
- You share a common vision.
- You experience true intimacy.

CREATING YOUR ROMANTIC DESTINY

Designing and creating your romantic destiny is a conscious act that begins with self-awareness and intention. It's about making choices that align with your values and goals rather than simply reacting to circumstances or settling for less than you deserve. When you approach your relationships with this level of intentionality, you are actively shaping the course of your love life and setting the stage for a fulfilling future.

STEPPING INTO YOUR FUTURE

As you move forward, remember that compatibility is not just about finding someone who fits into your life—it's about creating a life that aligns with who you truly are. The journey of understanding compatibility and consciously designing your romantic destiny is also a journey of self-discovery, growth, and empowerment.

You are no longer living under the weight of your past relationships. Your confidence increases because you trust yourself more as you are moving toward the future of your dreams. With each step you take, you are becoming the woman you were always meant to be: strong, confident, and in control of your destiny. As you continue to embrace this journey, you will find that the love and happiness you seek are already within you, waiting to be shared with a partner who is truly compatible with the woman you have become.

This chapter provides a foundational taste of the principles and practices that can help women cultivate their destiny relationship—one that is not only fulfilling but also aligned with their deepest values and true selves.

CREATE A NEW REALITY

As you redefine your identity, you also begin to create a new reality for yourself. This new reality is not something that happens by chance—it is something you consciously design.

KEY MESSAGES

1. **The power of vision.** A clear vision is essential for creating the relationship of your dreams. By understanding your core values, past experiences, and what you truly desire in a partner, you can set the stage for a relationship that supports your growth and happiness.
2. **Breaking free from shame-based beliefs.** Your beliefs shape your reality. By identifying and transforming your barriers, you're opening up new possibilities for love and

fulfillment. This process of breaking free allows you to live authentically and attract a partner who resonates with your highest potential.

3. **Understanding compatibility.** Compatibility is the cornerstone of a successful relationship. It's about aligning core values, life goals, emotional needs, and communication styles. By understanding and assessing compatibility, you can build a relationship that is resilient, meaningful, and capable of withstanding the test of time.

4. **Consciously creating your romantic destiny.** The journey to your dream relationship is a conscious one involving intentional choices and self-awareness. As you design your romantic destiny, you are also becoming the woman you were always meant to be: confident, empowered, and living in alignment with your true self.

My transformational coaching program is designed specifically for successful, professional women like you who are ready to break the cycle of unfulfilling relationships and step into a partnership that matches the life they've built. It offers women the tools and insights they need to cultivate a relationship that is not only fulfilling but also reflective of their true desires and values. This transformational journey empowers women to reclaim their power, build confidence, and create a relationship that supports their ongoing growth and fulfillment. By trusting in their journey and making intentional choices, women can step into their romantic destinies with clarity, purpose, and a deep sense of self-worth.

Imagine a future where you wake up each day with a profound sense of self-confidence, peace, and certainty. You are no longer burdened by the weight of past relationships, nor are you haunted by the fear of never finding true love. Instead, you carry with you the knowledge that you have the authentic power to shape your romantic destiny—a destiny that aligns with your deepest values and aspirations.

My clients go from feeling stuck and discouraged to empowered and confident. They break free from their past relationship patterns and find supportive, loving partners who celebrate their achievements and support their growth. This is not just a dream. It's the reality that awaits you when you commit to the six-month coaching program, "Conscious Love: Attracting and Creating Destiny Relationships."

WHAT THIS PROGRAM OFFERS

In this transformative journey, you will be guided step-by-step to attract and create the relationship you've always dreamed of. Imagine walking into every date or new connection with the certainty that you are choosing, not settling, leading you to the love and partnership you truly deserve. This program is designed to empower you to:

- **Cultivate unprecedented self-confidence.** No longer will you question your worth or settle for less than you deserve. Through personalized coaching, you will build a deep-seated self-confidence that radiates in all aspects of your life, attracting the right partner effortlessly.
- **Develop authentic power.** You will learn to harness your authentic power—the power to make intentional choices that align with your vision for love and life. This power will enable you to create and maintain a relationship that not only fulfills you but also supports your growth and evolution.
- **Embrace a bright future.** No matter how many broken relationships you've had before, this program will help you transform your past into a source of strength. You will cultivate a deep trust in your bright future, knowing that every step you take is leading you toward the relationship you were always meant to have.
- **Achieve peace of mind.** Through this journey, you will attain a sense of peace that comes from knowing you are in control of your destiny. The anxiety and fear of the unknown will be replaced by a calm present.
- **Become the woman you were meant to be.** Ultimately, this program is about becoming the best version of yourself. You will not only attract the partner of your dreams but also step fully into your power as the woman you were always

meant to be—strong, confident, and aligned with your true purpose.

GET READY TO TAKE THE NEXT STEP

Your journey toward attracting and creating your destiny relationship begins with a commitment to yourself. The six-month "Conscious Love" coaching program is your opportunity to step into a future filled with love, growth, and fulfillment. To leave the past behind and embrace the empowered, confident woman you are destined to become.

Are you ready to attract a partner who shares your passion for life, your values, and your vision for the future? Are you ready to create a relationship that supports your growth and brings out the best in you? Are you ready to live with the confidence, peace, and power that come from knowing you are in control of your romantic destiny?

If the answer is yes, then let's begin this transformative journey together. Your future, your love, and your life are waiting for you. Take the first step! Schedule a call with me today.

This chapter was designed to inspire and empower you as you embark on the journey to creating the relationship and life you've always dreamed of. Thank you for allowing me to be part of your journey. The best is yet to come.

To Your Greatness!

Klara Nemes Brown is a licensed psychotherapist, certified marriage and family therapist, certified EMDR therapist, relationship transformational coach, and best-selling author. She recently obtained a certification from Who's Who in America for professional integrity and outstanding achievement in her field and has made innumerable contributions to society as a whole.

Klara has been a dedicated private practice counselor and coach for over two decades. She is a long-time student of professional development and spiritual principles. Her passion lies in empowering women to thrive and reach their highest potential in life. She envisions a world where women boldly pursue their desires for growth and success in every area of their lives, unencumbered by social expectations and self-doubt. Currently, she lives in Lakeland, Florida, with her husband and her puppy.

For more information or to contact Klara

Facebook
www.facebook.com/klara.n.brown

—

LinkedIn
www.LinkedIn.com/in/klaranemesbrown/

—

Instagram
www.Instagram.com/klara.n.brown/

They Don't Test You...

ON THE THINGS THAT MATTER

By Kylie Burton, DC CFMP, FMS

My hands were shaking as I opened the computer. This was my second attempt at passing the National Board Part 3 Exams. The first attempt did not produce positive results, so I was back at the computer shaking as I was about to pull up my scores for round two.

I was alone with my two-month-old baby in my parents' basement. My little family had just moved back home to Utah from Oregon. I had completed my Doctorate of Chiropractic and was waiting to finish passing all the national board exams to get my license. From the start, I knew I was going to open my own practice. I knew next to nothing about business, but I would figure it out.

I remember this day very clearly and my eyes tear up just thinking about it. We had all prayed I could pass this test and move on with life. After four of the most difficult years of my life, I was ready to put school behind me and enter the next phase of life: motherhood and entrepreneur-hood.

But God had different plans for me, I guess. As I anticipated a positive result on this second attempt, I was met with the word "Failed." All that I had planned for 2017 went down the drain. I couldn't open my business without a license, and I couldn't get my license until I passed this dang test.

Tears came. I cried for hours that day. The first person I called was my mom, a teacher at a nearby elementary school. I went to her office, and she brought lunch so I could cry and eat privately.

All good mothers try to find the positive in a very ugly situation. I do that myself. However, this moment was different.

Why?

Why did college have to be so hard for me? High school was as easy as eating your favorite bowl of ice cream. College—I struggled!

Looking back, I had major testing anxiety. I just didn't realize that's what it was back then. I'm the kind of girl who's going to power through and find a way no matter what. I did, but that doesn't mean it was easy.

In fact, during undergrad, I had such bad testing anxiety I would go to professors' offices and verbally take the tests with them. They wouldn't even provide me with multiple-choice answers. I'd just state the answer, and we'd move on. Graduate school didn't offer this—you either passed tests or got kicked out of the program. I almost got kicked out, too. The first test we took, three weeks into chiropractic school, I received a 68%. I needed a 70 to pass.

They would give you a warning, but then, on attempt number two, you either passed or were kicked out. You can believe I studied my heart out for my final attempt. I passed by the skin of my teeth with a 72%.

You see, it didn't matter how much I studied. The anxiety would kick in, and my mind would draw blanks. It was the worst when we were doing in-person skills with a classmate as a partner. One time, I had to perform muscle testing in front of an ornery old professor who thought he was the king of the world and mister know-it-all. I ran through all of the tests for each muscle with my partner before we entered the testing room and knew them all. The moment the door closed behind me, it was a different story.

"What happened in there?" My classmate asked after we had finished.

"I don't know. My mind blanked." I went home and cried again that day.

Why did testing have to be so hard for me? I knew the stuff.

So here I am: A new mommy with a desire to start my own business. I have a drive to move forward in life, and I've been stopped right in my path. I now have to take this test for the third time.

With this reality sinking in, I had to make a phone call—a good friend was planning to move back to Utah and be my assistant when I started this new business. We had worked together before, knew we worked well together and agreed on the business mission.

I picked up my phone and let it ring. We hadn't talked much over our 4-year hiatus as our lives took different ways. "Kelli," my voice was shaking, "Our timeline for opening this office has to change. I have to take this test again."

The phone call was pretty short, but she was understanding and altered her plans accordingly. Kelli and I started this business as a team at the beginning of 2018. She's still with me today, so I've done something right, even though our plans have pivoted on more than one occasion.

If you're a woman who feels the world has been stacked against you again and again—like I felt taking exam after exam—I wrote this for you.

Why? Because let me tell you what *I wasn't tested on*:

- Nobody ever tested me on my ability to run a business.
- Nobody ever tested me on my leadership skills.
- Nobody ever tested me on my tenacity.
- Nobody ever tested me on my ability to care, to teach, or to change others' lives.
- Nobody ever tested me on my ability to market myself and my expertise.
- Nobody ever tested me on my ability to show up live in front of a camera.
- Nobody ever tested me on my drive to be a better mom, wife, and boss.
- Nobody ever tested me on my relationship with money.
- Nobody ever tested me on my ability to share my expertise on podcasts.
- Nobody ever tested my courage to take risks.

I could keep going, but you get the picture. What we are tested on doesn't determine our destiny in the real world. I always say, "I have an expensive piece of paper. What I do with it is up to me." The paper does not dictate our future. We do.

Can I share five keys that have helped me dictate my life so you can feel limitless, too?

KEY #1: ALLOW YOUR DREAMS TO EVOLVE

When I first opened my practice, once I finally passed the test (on attempt number three), I envisioned a giant brick-and-mortar office space with daycare so moms could drop off their kids and receive wellness/spa-like care without having to watch the kiddos with their third eye.

In 2019, I was sick with a pregnancy and living on IV therapy. I couldn't physically get to our little 400-square-foot office room, so we called it quits. Within two weeks of making the decision, Kelli and I transitioned the business to be completely virtual. Little did we know what would happen less than six months later in 2020.

When the world flipped upside down, I was already virtual. How does a chiropractor take their skills to a virtual platform? Blood work. The regular blood work that people get from their doctor's office. At this point in my journey, I have helped people who were repeatedly told their blood work was normal, yet still felt terrible, find real answers, healing, and hope. So, blood work was my ticket to running a virtual business.

Doors began opening. I walked through them even though I knew little ol' me could barely pass exams, and I had to take the most important ones multiple times. One of these opportunities changed the trajectory of my business: I started teaching my colleagues how to do what I was doing inside a Facebook group.

Wait... I went from treating patients to business and clinical consulting in nearly a blink of an eye. When I did, I found my passion. Yes, I was good at patient care. But I was even better at consulting colleagues and helping them grow their businesses.

These opportunities have helped my dreams evolve. I literally run a seven-figure business from a bedroom in my house. My little kids (I now have three) pop in on my Zoom camera and say "hi" often. It's the norm for so many of us. How grateful we should be for the opportunities that have arisen!

Remember those tests I really struggled with? I was tested on my ability to regurgitate information they figured was relevant (and in the way they thought I should regurgitate it). What they didn't test me on was my ability to host a three-hour Zoom workshop with over 250 of my colleagues in attendance and have them invest in my programs before the Zoom session even ended. Nope, that was never a test question.

So next time you think, *Who am I to...* Remember, if I can, you can. The next time your dreams change, welcome the change! Allow it and know that you can have it all. You get the *and* in life: Wife, Mother, *and* Boss Babe.

If I can, you can. You are a Limitless Woman, too.

KEY #2: KISS YOUR TIMELINES GOODBYE

The week before I got married, I took 26 exams. 26 exams in 6 days!!

Yes, it's absurd. Yes, we've been conditioned to have strict timelines and to always meet them. Then, instead of celebrating what we just did and accomplished, it's off to the next one. Next test. Next semester. Next school year. Next degree. Next certification.

It's wrong. And it nearly destroyed me.

My ability to be present as a mom, wife, and leader has been hindered because I've been trained to set strict and impossible timelines for myself. If I didn't meet them, shame on me—I failed.

Let me give you an example. Every January, we business owners set a goal for the total revenue we want to achieve in the upcoming year. When I was working towards a seven-figure business, that was my goal: hit seven figures within the year.

Here's the timeline problem: I didn't hit it my first year that it was my goal. Nor did I hit it in my second year of the goal. So, instead of celebrating the $750,000 I did in revenue that year, I felt like a failure because I didn't hit the seven figures.

I didn't hit seven figures within the timeline I had placed on myself, so I felt like a failure! Newsflash: Less than 2 percent of women entrepreneurs ever hit seven figures! Here I am expecting myself to do something very few can actually accomplish. I imagine less than 1 percent of women owners with kids can accomplish $750,000, and I'm over here doing it with babies acting like it's nothing.

See what I mean? All these tests, the degrees, and the never-ending "it's not enough" have nearly destroyed me. I should've been celebrating the $750,000 in revenue and not feeling like a failure because I didn't hit the big seven-figure number!

Can I give you a challenge? Remove all timelines from your goals. Notice when you do this, how much freer you feel?

Let me give you another example.

As I participate in this book, I'm also writing my own solo book. I've got giant plans for this thing. And typical me, I started it and placed a strict timeline on my desired date for completion and launch.

Two months in, I learned this lesson again: Remove all timelines and watch what happens when you're just in the flow.

When the pivoting point occurred, I had outlined the whole book and was well into the first three chapters but couldn't figure out a title. We had a vague idea of the subtitle but knew it wasn't it. If you've ever had the feeling of knowing when you nailed something, you get what I mean. That feeling hadn't arrived yet—until I released the timeline from myself.

I literally said out loud, "I'll finish this book and launch it when I'm ready." That was it. I released the timeline for my team and me.

The title and subtitle came to my mind the next day, literally. In fact, my business's new brand came the next day. My seven-figure brand was turned into an eight-figure new idea, but it didn't flow until I released the timeline I had placed on myself.

If you're like me and you're used to timelines placed upon us by others, and you're notorious for placing them on yourself, please stop. It has nearly destroyed me on more than one occasion.

Do it for yourself. Do it for those you love and watch as your relationships improve and you have your best ideas yet!

KEY #3: HIRE HELP

Guilty. That's the feeling I had the first several times someone came to clean my house. Guilty is how I felt getting HelloFresh shipped to my doorstep, so at least the hardest question of the day was answered three times a week, "Mom, what's for dinner?" Guilty is how I felt going out for dinner multiple times a week.

Society makes us women feel guilty. We should be able to do everything. We should be able to help support the income, cook dinner, read bedtime stories at night, and keep our sanity through it all.

Should.

This isn't reality.

I get my house cleaned every three weeks and it's what helps me stay sane. I no longer judge myself for ordering Applebee's or Texas Roadhouse for dinner when I killed it that day in sales or when I've been working on a new offer all day.

If I can have help around the house, even when it's hired, I get to be more present with kids when I'm not at work. I'm totally okay with this. So, if you know how I can hire someone to do my laundry, I'm game for it, too.

What help can you hire to take a load off your shoulders? It's worth the investment as it allows you to spend your time elsewhere—on your business or with your kiddos and be fully present.

What would provide you the most relief? If it's getting your house cleaned, make a phone call. If it's having a meal kit ordered at home, get online and find one that appeals to you. I've tried several, and I like rotating them just for greater variety. Maybe it's investing in a $100 nap every three weeks by getting your lashes done or your toenails painted. Whatever it is, you're worth it. By the way, I have a $100 nap when I get my eyelashes done, and it's the best $100 I have spent.

You can be limitless. But there's not an unlimited amount of time for us to do all the things. Let others help you. You're investing in their small business, too.

KEY #4: YOU 2.0

For what feels like forever, even though it's only been the last two years, I wanted to leave what people have known me for: bloodwork girl. Bloodwork girl is me, version 1.0. Functional Blood Work Specialist was my signature program, which I created as version 1.0 me.

Version 2.0 me is a boss babe known for her marketing, sales, and top-of-funnel genius. Version 2.0 me is the CEO of my new company: Foundational Medicine Institute.

Version 1.0 me is the author of the book *Why Are My Labs Normal?* Version 2.0 me is the author of the book *Foundational Medicine: The Business Blueprint for Serving 10,000 Patients.*

See the difference? I'm grateful for both versions of me because 2.0 me would not exist without version 1.0 me.

What does version 2.0 look like for you?

First, you have to create it in your mind. Go to YouTube and search for a "1:47 timer." Pick a video with background music for one minute and 47 seconds. Go somewhere quiet where you can think and not be disturbed.

Click play and close your eyes.

What do you see your version 2.0 doing? You've got one minute and 47 seconds to create it in your mind.

Let me tell you what I saw the first time I did this.

I'm married to a hard worker. Every summer, he spends thousands of hours roofing. For the last few years, he's been running his own business (yes, we run multiple businesses out of our house). He's never been able to play during the summer for the last 20 years of his life. Roofing consumes his summers.

My goal in business was to buy his time back. The version 2.0 me was the boss babe making enough to not only provide for the family but also to have plenty extra. I love vacations and traveling, so we needed more than enough to survive. We needed that and more (for my vacations).

In my minute and forty-seven seconds, I saw a year when we lived in a new, beautiful white and black house with plenty of space and a pool in the backyard. I envisioned taking multiple vacations this same year and playing often during the summer without the stress of work.

Once I saw this in my mind, I figured out what to do to make it happen. You better believe I've done all the things. I've taken every risk I could possibly take—risks like investing in a $60,000 mentorship program when I only had $26,000 in the bank. I've put myself out there and had things not go my way more often than they have. I've persevered through being $165,000 in the hole (from a risk that went south pretty quickly). And I've come out on top.

This year was the year I saw in my mind. We live in our new white and black house with plenty of space. The pool plans are being finalized as we speak (in addition to a shop that'll serve as my new office space upstairs). As a family, we've gone to Cancun not once but twice. Disney World is the next destination. Plus, this was the first summer in 20 years my husband didn't have to worry about selling and putting on roofs. He experienced a stress-free summer—the first in his life!

I was successful in creating version 2.0 me. (Now I need to return to the 1:47 video and create version 3.0.)

If I can, you can. You are a Limitless Woman, too.

KEY #5: GET COMFORTABLE WITH LOSS

As you grow into the 2.0 version of you, you're going to experience loss along the way—at least you should if you're doing it right. You see, you can't share your dreams with people who aren't dreamers. You also can't be friends with people who are jealous of what you have or place negative judgments about what you're going after. Now that you've done your minute and 47-second challenge and you know your vision for your life, you had better be careful who you share it with.

I look back at my life, and it's actually very rare for someone to have spent longer than four years with me. Outside of family members, I can identify two people at this point: my husband and my assistant, Kelli (whom I've previously mentioned). Even in my youth, nobody ever lasted longer than four years with me. I don't have that friend "who I've been friends with for 20 years."

Growing up, I was picked on, pointed at, and never really fit in. At the time, I figured it was me who had the problem. I've come to learn that I was never made to fit in. I was never made to participate and remain at the same level in life for very long. I'm constantly growing, constantly dreaming, and constantly doing the things necessary for my dreams to become my reality. I wish I realized this growing up when I never got the leadership role in my church group, when I was shunned from the "cool kids club" in sixth grade, or when I wasn't invited to hang out with my teammates on the weekends.

I was different. I wasn't crazy. I was just first—first in the group I was in.

Being first doesn't mean you're crazy. It just means you need to change your network. You need a new group to be in.

Let's flash back to the end of 2020. I had always made excuses on why I couldn't "network." This momma had boundaries, and going to dinner and networking events in the evenings crossed those boundaries.

But in 2020, the world shifted, and suddenly, there were a zillion networking groups online! I joined my first one that fall—a paid group where every participant invested in being there. Four years later, I'm still in this group. It's been absolutely priceless. I've attended Zoom meetings as much as possible and flown across the country and back in less than 24 hours simply to be in the same room as my new friends—the people who get me.

I remember one specific weekend when I got invited to an exclusive event. This event filled my soul. I told the leader and host I was so grateful for this space she had created because my friends were at this table, in this room.

Find those who fuel your fire, fill your soul, and support your audacious moves as you become You 2.0. Yes, that means you need to get comfortable with loss. As I said, nobody has ever stayed in my life for more than four years. It's not a bad thing. It's just my reality.

Be so dedicated to becoming You 2.0 that those lost relationships create spaces for new ones—the ones with people who say "Jump" when you tell them that crazy idea or the next-level business model you're crafting. The friends who encourage you to chase the next dream and say, "You got this! Go for it!"

I'll be your first new friend. We will get in that airplane together and continue to jump without a parachute even as it climbs to a higher and higher altitude. Why? Because we will both do the things necessary to become our version 2.0 (and 3.0 and 4.0).

CONCLUSION

Imposter syndrome? Self-doubt? Kick that crap to the curb. This girl barely passed her college exams. I failed my boards not once but twice!

They never tested me on what's actually required in business to not just survive but thrive. They never tested me on my ability to mother my kids. They never tested me on my ability to be a wife and have a thriving marriage at the same time as we both run our own businesses.

Chances are, you've never been tested on these either. There's no test for determining if you're a Limitless Woman. I am. If you're reading this, so are you. The only person that would've stopped me is me. The only person who could stop you is the person you see looking back at you in the mirror.

The world needs more Limitless Women. Women who know we are limitless have the *and* in life. If you want more *and* in your life, I'd be happy to help, especially if you're in the alternative healthcare space and/or interested in running a virtual practice.

I'm Dr. Kylie Burton, the chiropractor who hates adjusting, and I'm your biggest cheerleader.

Dr. Kylie Burton is a chiropractor who hates adjusting. As a mom, she knew she needed to abandon the traditional healthcare model so she could onboard hundreds at a time. This would allow her to have the *and* in life, be a mom *and* "boss babe." Now, she teaches her colleagues how to do the same.

Dr. Kylie is a five-time #1 best-selling author, hosts two top-rated podcasts, and is a serial "mompreneur."

As the founder of the Foundational Medicine Institute and the 10,000 Patients Framework, she has amplified the businesses of thousands of her colleagues who are ready to break free of the one-to-one trap and enter the world of time freedom, allowing all to be more present for the ones they love the most.

Dr. Kylie has been seen on *Good Morning Utah, Fox 26 Houston, The List* (which aired nationally on ABC, NBC, and CBS), and seven international radio talk shows.

To learn more, go to
Sprint.drkylieburton.com

—

And listen to her podcasts
Beyond the Diagnosis
10,000 Patients

Fearless Success

OVERCOMING FEAR TO ACHIEVE YOUR GREATEST POTENTIAL

By Monika Hengesbach, EA

Life has not been easy, and many times, I just wanted to get off this spinning world and never get back on. However, I am grateful I stayed. Through faith and perseverance, I have overcome a lot, and I am a much stronger and better version of my previous self. I have always believed there is a reason and a purpose for what we go through, and I hope that my experience can help someone else from feeling that it is only happening to them. My chapter is geared toward all entrepreneurs in all stages of their business—from infancy to closure—who just need to know what they feel is "normal" (if there is such a thing).

REMOVE YOURSELF

I remember when I first started my tax practice. I was a single mom with a 2-year-old living off my credit cards, and my mom was living with me to help me with my daughter. I knew how to do taxes and accounting but knew absolutely nothing about networking. One day, I met with a banker to see how we could refer business to each other, and I started to cry. I felt I was doing everything wrong for my family. She pointed across the street to McDonald's and said, "Can you get a job there?"

I was appalled! How dare you think I would. Of course, I could.

She said, "Why are you crying?"

BAM! It hit me! I was so fixated on the idea of where I felt I should be, what I perceived to be a failure, that I didn't realize I was exactly where I was supposed to be. As entrepreneurs, we believe that as soon as we hang the shingle on the front door, business will flock in, and we will be an overnight success. When it doesn't, we immediately blame ourselves as if we did something wrong. We have gotten in the way of our own success. All we need to do is stay focused on the present. Easier said than done, I know. When you do, you are better equipped to listen and learn. After the meeting with the banker, I took myself out of the equation, and the doors opened. I accepted the process and lived in the present moment. I was now ready to listen and open to learning.

YOU ARE NOT ALONE

A friend had asked me to go out for drinks. I told her that between taking care of my mom, running a business, and raising my daughter, I needed time to clean my house.

She asked, "How long does it take you to clean your house?"

I told her a whole Saturday as I hated cleaning my home.

"Why don't you hire a maid?"

Hire a maid. Only the uber-rich can do that. She then told me to take what I bill my clients hourly and multiply that by the eight hours it takes me. Then factor in the cost of a maid. Was I ahead? I couldn't afford *not* to hire a maid.

As entrepreneurs, we always feel that we need to do everything. I don't know how many times I have heard from new entrepreneurs and mom-and-pop business owners that they can do their own bookkeeping and that their own taxes are not complicated enough to hire a professional. These entrepreneurs are more inclined to come from a scarcity mindset: that obsession that you are lacking something, and you can't seem to focus on anything other than that, no matter how hard you try.

That mindset is overwhelming and can choke the life out of your business and your energy. The entrepreneurial path can, at times, be a turbulent one. Sometimes, we need a life preserver to navigate these waters. *People want to help!* By outsourcing tasks that do not generate revenue, we free up time to focus on those that do. Not to mention the most priceless resource of all—our time. As Steve Jobs said, "It's really clear that the most precious resource we all have is time."

DON'T BE AFRAID OF THE NUMBERS

"Oh my God, I am going to owe a ton to Uncle Sam!" "I need to spend a ton because the government is not going to get another penny of my money." If I could tell you how many times I have heard those phrases from prospective clients, I would be a *very* rich woman. Is it important to know your bottom line? Yes. However, it is *not* important to fixate on the bottom line. Once we let the numbers take hold, we neglect our long-term goals and strategies, overlook opportunities for growth, and start to focus on the short-term, which leads to hasty decisions. Yes, buying a new car for your business is a great write-off in the first year, but what about the remaining years? Do you plan on being as profitable? And do you really need a new car, higher car insurance, and the dreaded car payment? Fear takes hold, and we start to do things that sabotage our own success.

Once we let go of the fear surrounding the numbers we are able to seek advice. A simple strategy session with a tax strategist can give you the right tools to help conquer your fear surrounding taxes and make the numbers work for you.

YOU DON'T HAVE TO KNOW WHO YOU ARE

How many times have you heard that before you can be successful, you need to know who you are? I don't know how many self-help books I have read where the foundation is based on that idea alone. What if you are that person who does not know who you are? Does that mean you are destined to fail? No. Throughout our lives, we encounter various lessons, whether it is through formal education, personal relationships, or challenges we face. Learning helps us grow and adapt to the world around us. When you put so much pressure upon yourself to have everything figured out, you are holding yourself to an unrealized expectation. Many successful individuals discover their identity and values along the way. It's possible to achieve success while still exploring who you are as long as you remain open to growth and learning. Ultimately, both self-awareness and the willingness to adapt play essential roles in one's journey to success. Learning is a lifelong journey.

EXPECT THE UNEXPECTED

After working in my own tax practice for five years, my business was growing. I became an expert in all things small business, especially in regard to real estate investing/strategy. My business was booming. Then, the real estate market crashed, and my mom had her first of many strokes. I was living in a two-story house approximately an hour away from my mother's doctors. I had to move. I lost my home, I lost clients, and my revenue dropped. I could have let this ruin me. Instead, I was grateful that I had the opportunity to be there for my mom when she transitioned from this life to the next. After the passing of my mom, I met someone, got married, and moved from California to Texas to start all over again. My practice once again was booming. I was back and even better than before. Then *BAM!* COVID hit, and a year after that, my marriage ended. An empty nester at the age of 56, I was once again starting over. What? This is not what I planned.

Once again, I could've let this destroy me. Looking back, this was the best thing that ever happened to me. I found out that all the parts of me that I thought were healed were indeed only duct taped, and when my marriage ended, I unraveled. It was through this process that I began the arduous journey of learning about myself, my likes, dislikes, etc. I can honestly say that I am a healthier and better version of my previous self. Life is unpredictable; even if you feel like you have everything under control, unexpected things happen. As entrepreneurs, we need to be mentally flexible and ready to handle anything that comes our way.

We need to embrace flexibility and be open to pivot at a moment's notice. We need to diversify our risk and not put all our eggs in one basket (such as only specializing in real estate). We need to save for emergencies and have a contingent plan. We need to have a strong network of advisors and mentors who can offer us support and guidance. We need to communicate openly with our team, customers, and shareholders. This builds trust and aligns us with our brand. And finally, we need to learn and evolve. We need to look at unexpected challenges not as obstacles but as learning experiences. We can turn surprises into opportunities and navigate troubled waters with greater confidence and success.

"The only thing standing between you and your goal is the story you keep telling yourself as to why you can't achieve it."
~Jordan Belfort

I want to thank you all for reading my chapter. I hope and pray that my experiences have given you faith that you are not alone.

Monika Hengesbach is an Enrolled Agent, NTPI Fellow, Concierge Certified Tax Advisor, and CEO of Decision Financial Services, Inc, where she specializes in tax strategies for individuals and small to midsize businesses. With over 20 years of experience in the tax industry, Monika has helped clients improve their tax strategies, minimize liabilities, and help clients navigate the complexity of today's tax code.

Monika has been interviewed by a variety of news talk radio shows discussing all things financial and has been published in *MSN Finance, Haro Banking,* and *Buzzfeed*. She is passionate about helping her clients achieve long-term success by saving money on taxes! She currently is working on her own nonprofit, L.I.F.E. (Living in Financial Excellence) Happens! which helps educate women and young adults to be financially savvy. In her free time, you can either find her playing a competitive game of pickleball or hanging out with her daughter.

You can connect with Monika via her podcast
The Wealthy Wallet
https://www.linkedin.com/company/decisionfinancialservicesinc/
—

Facebook
https://www.facebook.com/decisionfinancial

A Journey of Faith

FINDING PEACE, PURPOSE, AND LIGHT IN THE DARKNESS

By Rasika Salva

When asked, "What does success look like?" it's easy to answer with a list that includes achievements, societal or career status, and monetary wealth. They are most definitely a given by worldly standards. And if you are on a path to conquer all of those, then I hope that you will be immensely blessed. But I'm here today to offer a different perspective and share with you that success also lies in something that transcends the material gains of this world and connects us to a dimension that holds a power and a sense of peace that is sometimes beyond human comprehension.

My journey in personal and spiritual growth began years ago, but it was not fully realized until the last few years. Looking back now, I recognize that I was already shifting in my early twenties, although I had a long way to go, with plenty of misguided ideologies to work through and mistakes to make. What I want to share with you today are the important lessons that I was forced to confront and learn from during one of the most difficult times in my life—what I would describe as a parent's worst nightmare. It is true that tough times teach us a lot about ourselves if we are open to it, and this experience that I will share certainly did that and more.

I can tell you that if someone had told me ahead of time what I was about to experience, I would have vehemently said, "Absolutely not! There is *no* way I can survive it!" Yet, here I am almost three years later, and I am on the proverbial "other side." No, it is not all sunshine and roses; life never is. But my life is filled with gratitude, strength, hope, and unwavering faith.

No matter where you are in your spiritual growth, I hope that you keep reading this chapter with an open mind and receptive heart. If you are not ready for this chapter yet, I completely respect that, and I wish you all the best in the hopes that one day, you will circle back here when you are ready for this step in your life's journey.

Here's the thing: I believe there are no accidents, and therefore, I believe this chapter didn't randomly come into your life. So, even if you're not completely sure you're ready to dive into this part of your personal growth, I urge you to simply try. Take that first step today, and know that you are reading these words for a reason.

If you choose to keep reading, then I applaud you. I pray that you will gain inspiration as you read these reflections and pause to look back on your own journey to this very moment. And I pray that you will find opportunities to end this chapter with a renewed sense of faith and understanding of a greater purpose in your life. So with that said, open your heart and come on this walk with me.

WHEN HE SPEAKS

I was 34 months pregnant with our first boy. My husband, Skyler, and I already had a beautiful three-year-old girl, Alexcia, and now we were about to have one of each. We had won the lottery. The nursery was prepared, and all the registry gifts were ready and waiting. I happily made my way to my OB appointment, anxious to hear an update on my son. As usual, my belly growth was measured so we could notate how well he was growing. "Hmm, no change," said the practitioner. I was surprised. As I reflected back on my first pregnancy, I remembered never hearing that during my third trimester. I was put at ease and told not to worry. I sighed with relief, put it out of my mind, and trusted everything was alright.

I returned the next week. Again, there was no change in growth. Now, I began to worry. Once more, my practitioner assured me I had nothing to worry about. "Every pregnancy is different," they said. I had also laid off all sugars during that time to help control my glucose, so I rationalized that perhaps I just wasn't packing on as much size anymore. I still fought with myself, though, because I could not shake a nagging feeling in my stomach.

At 37 weeks, I went on my next visit. This time, my belly measured smaller. I began to panic. The practitioner moved me to a room to perform a non-stress test. The results came back normal, but I wasn't convinced. I demanded an ultrasound to get a closer look. I was told to come back the following week if it would help me feel more at ease, but I was reassured the non-stress test proved everything was fine. I walked out of the building feeling uneasy. I shared my worry with Skyler, and we called his mother for advice. My mother-in-law gave me the confidence to trust my gut feeling, not to wait a whole week for an ultrasound, and head immediately to the emergency room.

I went to the hospital and was checked in for a non-emergency maternity visit. I remember sitting in the waiting room as I watched one expectant mother after another get wheeled in. Despite the potential lack of fetal growth for the past three weeks, I was not cataloged as an emergency patient, so I was not considered a priority case. Finally, after 3-1/2 hours, I was brought back to do an ultrasound. Now, if you have ever had to get imaging done, you are probably aware that ultrasound techs are known for having the best poker faces. But as I watched this tech intently, I could actually see the look in her eyes change as she took the images. She walked me to a patient room with a bed, and at that moment, I knew I was being admitted.

The attending OB walked in and asked me when I had eaten last. I had been so stressed out since my morning appointment that I hadn't eaten in eight hours. Having had a C-section with my first child, I knew why I was being asked this question. I just looked at the OB and said, "He's coming out today, isn't he?" The OB proceeded to explain that there was barely any amniotic fluid left, and my son was measuring smaller than normal. He was in real danger of stillbirth if we delayed any further. As I listened to the doctor explain this, I felt my heart in my throat. What if I had waited until next week? What if I had forced myself to quiet the voice inside that was yelling, "SOS?"

The surgery went well, and our son was finally out, safe and sound. Skyler had arrived just before I was taken to the OR, and we were anxious to hear our son's voice. Logan Kayde Salva was born at 37 weeks, weighing five pounds and two ounces. He was perfect. He was tiny and swam in every newborn onesie we had. He couldn't be transported home in a regular car seat, as he failed the car seat test three times. But we were graciously provided with a car bed specifically designed for preemies.

The following few weeks were normal, except that Logan had newborn jaundice. We had not experienced that with our daughter but were told it was perfectly normal, especially because Logan was a preemie. We were given a prescription for regular, gentle sunlight every day, and all was expected to resolve itself.

Granted, Logan's complexion changed a bit with regular sunshine, and we get plenty of it here in Florida. After four weeks, however, I couldn't help but feel that something was off. I remember staring at him and studying his skin and eyes. I didn't know what I was looking for, but I knew I was looking for something. I began to vocalize my confusion; his complexion just seemed off somehow.

Now, to clarify, Skyler and I are an interracial couple. I'm East Indian, and he is of mostly German, Irish, and Norwegian descent. Darker complexions usually develop over time in the first year of life. Logan, however, looked oddly tan, as if someone had spread a light layer of self-tanner around his cheeks, arms, and legs. I remember Skyler telling me it was probably the warm lighting in our home, and at the time, I figured maybe he was right. I knew I was still hormonal in that postpartum phase, so I thought, *Maybe he's right. Maybe I really am just imagining things.*

Four weeks turned into eight, and on the day of Logan's two-month wellness visit, his complexion was definitely darker. I couldn't stop seeing a golden undertone in his skin that left me incredibly uneasy. As soon as his pediatrician walked into the exam room, I greeted her with,

"Am I crazy, or is he looking yellow?" She stopped, at first surprised by my abrupt greeting, I think, and then I saw her start to see it, too. We were quickly sent to our local hospital for labs, and within two hours, we received a call. Before she even said it, I could hear it in her voice. The voice doctors use when they are about to deliver news that will wreck your world. The words no parent should ever have to hear, "It's his liver."

Those three words punched me in my gut. I felt sick to my stomach, and my heart began to race. I knew. I had known all along. Every time I scanned his face and eyes. Deep down, I knew. But I didn't know to trust myself. I didn't know that my intuition was right. I had sought validation outside of myself because I didn't believe. Because of that, weeks had gone by. I felt overwhelming guilt. I had failed my baby. It was my job to protect him, but I hesitated because I didn't know how to listen to my inner voice.

Both of these stories serve as an example of how incredibly important it is to trust your intuition. At the time, I was just beginning to discover this, but our intuition is more than our inner guide. As you continue to read, I will share more events on this journey that transformed my understanding of how deeply connected we all are to a greater divine force, whether we are awake to that realization yet or not. As a Christian, I believe we are all connected to God through our divine souls.

Your intuition is how God speaks to you. It is a language that is unheard by others but specifically designed for you in moments of need. Full disclosure: At that time, I hadn't quite grasped this concept. I believed in God, but I didn't know just how close He could be. I didn't know how to pray or engage in a personal relationship with Him. The only times I prayed were when the pastor or preacher told the congregation to do so during church, and I can tell you I often didn't know how to verbalize my prayers. I hadn't yet discovered just how connected I could be to God and how prayer doesn't have to come in any special form, only that it needs to be ultimately sincere and embrace vulnerability, shedding all pretenses and ego.

Now, I understand that intuition guides and nudges us toward the path we need to follow because it is not random, but instead, it is divinely derived. By listening to it, you can align yourself with God's greater plan for you. I can also promise you that His plan for you is bigger and more intricate than you can possibly imagine and often defies logic. When you face doubt or when your own mortal logic is insufficient, I encourage you to lift your face and heart up to a much greater source of wisdom, one that is eternal and already knew you before you were born. Recognize it and honor it because it is God's voice guiding you.

AT HIS FEET

So there I was, being catapulted onto a road that was going to challenge me in ways I could never have imagined. My head was spinning with questions. I had no answers, and all I could think of was *Why Logan? Why an innocent two-month-old baby?* It would be a long time before I ever gained clarity on that question, and so, for the moment, I was simply reeling.

Logan was admitted to a reputable hospital in the Orlando area, where we were met with specialist after specialist. He was being put through a battery of tests, including a liver biopsy. Minutes felt like hours, and hours felt like days, especially as I waited for test results. I desperately hoped that with each new test, we would finally have definitive results that could give us a plan. But instead, they only confirmed that Logan's liver was seriously compromised and left everyone with more questions as to why. Eventually, he was examined by one of the country's top Pediatric GI specialists. With one look at Logan, he said, "I think I know what this is, but I need confirmation." So we were once again thrown into a barrage of tests, x-rays, EKGs, echocardiograms, and liver ultrasounds. In addition, both my husband and I were asked to submit blood samples to test our genomes against Logan's. And then, we were told to wait again.

A few days turned into a week, and we still had no answers. I could feel myself breaking. I couldn't help my son. He was so small and helpless, lying in his hospital crib with IV lines and constant poking and prodding. I was desperate for control, and I felt like the more I was trying to grasp control, the faster it was slipping out of my fingers. Two surgeons walked in and sat me down. *It can't be good if they're making me sit down,* I thought to myself. They were convinced that Logan had biliary atresia. "Biliary atresia is a disease of the bile ducts that affects only infants."[1] Basically, bile ducts become inflamed, causing blockage and preventing the natural expulsion of bile from the body. When bile backs up into the liver, it damages it quite quickly, leading to cirrhosis, also known as fibrosis or scarring of the liver.

The surgeons continued to explain that there was no cure for this condition. There was a surgical procedure they were strongly recommending I consent to, even though it was risky, would only be a temporary band-aid, and would also expedite his need for a transplant. At that moment, I remember their voices becoming muffled by my raging thoughts of anguish and fear. I wanted to throw up. I remember signing consent forms for the surgery to happen in three days if no other diagnosis was made. I could barely see through my tears. There was now a ticking clock to get solid answers, and time was running out.

That night, I couldn't sleep. Honestly, I hadn't slept since we arrived except for the few hours a day when I just couldn't keep my eyes open anymore. I never left Logan's bedside. It was three o'clock in the morning. I was standing right next to his crib with one hand on his forehead and the other over his small belly. The whole floor was quiet, and I focused on the sound of his breathing. I could feel his little tummy move up and down gently underneath my hand. I thought how beautiful that sensation was. And then, it happened. I could hear something inside of me snap, and that's when I broke into what felt like a million pieces.

It all came pouring out of me. All the panic, anxiety, sorrow, grief, heartache, and sheer fear that I had been building up. It flooded out. I had been so desperate to hold on to any shred of control, but it was actually killing me piece by piece. The next thing I knew, words were coming out of my mouth, and I spoke them aloud right next to Logan as he continued to sleep. I had never spontaneously prayed, I had never

---

1. Biliary atresia: Facts & Symptoms. American Liver Foundation. Accessed October 1, 2024. https://liverfoundation.org/liver-diseases/pediatric-liver-information-center/pediatric-liver-disease/biliary-atresia/.

spoken to God from my heart, but I knew I had hit rock bottom. "Please, please help my son. I can't save him. I can't help him. His life is yours. I give it to You. He belongs to You. I give it all to You. His life. His destiny. Everything." I repeated these words over and over and over again.

With each repetition, I could feel my trembling subside. My turmoil slowly transformed to calm, my breath slowed down, and a rush of warmth spread from my back down to my arms and into my hands, which were still lying on Logan's head and abdomen. To this day, I still cannot explain what that was, but I can tell you it felt like the most powerful, warm, and secure embrace that seemed to permeate through me and into Logan.

I opened my eyes. Logan was still perfectly asleep. I felt at peace. I knew Logan was still in trouble, but I somehow felt peace. I looked at the clock in the room and an hour had gone by. I had prayed for an hour straight. I had completely surrendered all control to His will, and I felt my spirit was vibrating at a level I had never experienced before. I couldn't have put it into words at the time, as it was such a foreign feeling. Today, I describe it as a feeling of wholeness, of being rooted so deeply, a steadfastness that could not be shaken. It was a knowing. I didn't understand how, but I knew that somehow, God had Logan securely in His hands from that moment. I had finally chosen to let go.

Ten days had passed, and we finally had a diagnosis. Logan was born with the genetic mutation of Alagille syndrome (ALGS). "Alagille syndrome is an inherited condition in which bile builds up in the liver because there are too few bile ducts to drain the bile. This results in liver damage [...] It appears in one out of 70,000 babies and occurs in both sexes."[2] In addition to the liver, ALGS can also affect the kidneys, heart, and brain. The severity of symptoms can range from non-symptomatic to absolutely devastating. Because it is such a rare disease, there is not as much literature available on it as other congenital diseases. We had officially stepped into completely unknown territory. It was time for us to walk by faith.

---

2. Alagille Syndrome, Johns Hopkins Medicine, July 1, 2020, https://www.hopkinsmedi cine.org/health/conditions-and-diseases/alagille-syndrome.

Humans inherently crave control. It makes us feel powerful and, in some cases, invincible. But the truth is we all inevitably answer to one unwavering fact: We all die. None of us are exempt from this. No one has ever beaten death, except for one, because He is who He is. No amount of control in our lives will ever change the fact that we all have an expiration date, and when it is finally our time, nothing will stop it from happening. So, at the end of the day, our perception of control is just that: pure perception.

The word "perception" is defined as a belief or an opinion that many people share based on how things seem. How things seem is not fact. Sure, we can control what products we use, what foods we eat, and how healthy a lifestyle we choose to lead, but none of that ultimately changes whether we die or not, nor when. We have all heard stories of people who lead clean lives, never smoke, never drink, exercise regularly, and eat healthy, yet they still develop cancer. Some make it, and some don't. And in those moments, we find ourselves sitting there wondering how and why.

That one night in the hospital, I understood something that has become very fundamental to my faith today. I could not control whether my son would die or not. As a mother, I would do everything it took to sustain my son's health, jump through any hoop required, and make whatever sacrifice I needed to make. Ultimately, Logan's fate was not up to me or the many incredibly skilled specialists who would care for him.

When you find yourself in a moment of great need, embracing humility and completely surrendering to God's will is the ultimate step of faith you can take. It can be a terrifying step at first, but I can promise you the level of strength you can pull from God is beyond anything you can ever come up with on your own.

Understand something: Surrendering to God does not mean giving up. Instead, it means that we relinquish control of all of our darkest fears and give them to the highest power there is. He already knows your needs; He already knows what you are struggling with. He is just waiting for you to finally say, "Let *Your* will be done. Not mine, but Yours." If you choose to let go and allow God to take over your heart and your trials and tribulations, you will usher in waves upon waves of His divine wisdom, love, and guidance.

Jesus said, "Come to me, all you who are weary and burdened, and I will give you rest. Take my yoke upon you and learn from me, for I am gentle and humble in heart, and you will find rest for your souls. For my yoke is easy, and my burden is light" (Matthew 11:28–30). I encourage you to take the ultimate leap of faith today. If you are struggling in any way, big or small, or if you have depression or anxiety, suffer from addiction, or are still spinning from a medical diagnosis, surrender. Declare your submission to His will and His way. Whatever demons you are fighting in your life, raise your voice and make it known that your struggles are His; your fears are His.

You don't have to understand right away why you are going through it, whatever *it* is. When you give it to God, the answer to why will be revealed to you over time as it was to me. And it will always be shown to you when you are ready to receive it. God's timing is never wrong. Your ability to have courage and endurance through strife will prevail through your submission to His will. You may stumble from time to time because we are inevitably flawed humans. But He isn't. You can always draw on His strength by simply laying it all at His feet.

HIS PLAN A

It was a whole new world for us. In the first month, we quickly adjusted to managing multiple medications. We set up a whiteboard in our kitchen where we tracked daily dispensations and doses. We could not afford to make any mistakes. Logan also required specialized nutrition because his body could not process fats and fat-soluble vitamins. At the time, there was a shortage of baby formula in every store. We could only order his formula online and in bulk and often had to change suppliers due to shortages and supply chain issues.

The pressure to support our new lifestyle was increasing, so Skyler and I set a plan in action to drive me back into the workforce. I had acquired a position in management. I had a salary, commission, and full benefits. This was our Plan A. What I was not prepared for was how often I would have to go on leave for unforeseen hospitalizations.

Logan's immune system was compromised, and even a simple cold or unstable levels of Vitamin K could have him admitted for a week. My leave of absence became so frequent that HR had an ongoing open FMLA (Family and Medical Leave Act) for me whenever I needed it. Plan A was off to a bumpy start, to say the least.

To protect Logan's health, our life became home → work → home. We had lost all sense of knowing what to expect because there was no way to predict what would happen next. We were in a constant state of survival, a perpetual state of waiting for the other shoe to drop and praying for strength and mercy.

I was in sales at the time, and my work required me to be face-to-face with clients every day. Now, there is a crash course in maintaining high performance while your personal world is on fire. How do you genuinely find the strength to smile for others when you also want to cry from exhaustion? How do you open your heart to empathize with someone else's struggle when yours feels like it's ten thousand times greater? How do you set your ego aside and move forward with a servant's heart, putting others first throughout your day? I can promise you there wasn't a single part of this that I didn't struggle with, but it strengthened me to continue to lean on God even more.

Throughout this continuous daily faith, I somehow found genuine moments of happiness and levity. I found the empathy to recognize and honor that my family wasn't the only one in the world that was hurting. I managed to step outside myself and find reward in helping improve the lives of others. I found true gratitude. Little did I know how important practicing daily gratitude through prayer for even the smallest things would become.

Months went by, and after many more tests, Logan was finally approved to be listed for a transplant. There was renewed hope. Were our prayers going to be finally answered? The wait began for a deceased donor, but soon, three months of waiting turned into seven, and no potential matches were found. Logan's health was declining. He suffered from pruritus, also described as the liver itch. He'd scratch his legs, arms, hands, and feet until they bled and became sore. He began experiencing liver pain and would wake up in the middle of the night, every night, screaming from it. There were no peaceful nights.

I want to take a moment to recognize my husband for the many personal sacrifices he made during this time. Because Logan's needs had become too overwhelming overnight, he took it upon himself to move into Logan's room to ensure he would be right near him during those awful times, which had become a nightly event. Much sleep was lost, and many mornings started with back aches from sleeping on an air mattress next to Logan's crib. Alexcia had moved into our room, and I could tell she desperately needed comfort during those times as well. She clutched onto me all night. My heart goes out to all parents who are living through difficult situations like this. Not just parents of children with Alagille syndrome but all diseases and impactful disabilities. The parents often suffer in silence, masked by the brave faces we put on to protect our children, but it is all too real and cuts so very deeply.

Meanwhile, as the months passed, Logan's medical team kept stacking one new medication on top of another in the hopes of staving off organ failure a bit longer. His progressive jaundice was a cruel, constant reminder that Logan's life was finite, and the end of his was a lot closer than it should ever be for any child. We were watching our child slowly move closer to death. I wouldn't let myself think about next week, let alone next year. I just couldn't bring myself to do it. We would wake up and say, "Let's get him through today," and we would go to sleep saying, "Thank God, he made it through today." As much faith I had in God, I truly didn't know if Logan would make it to the age of two. Still, I made sure to practice gratitude every day.

I know that what I'm saying may seem incredulous to some. How could I possibly be grateful if I was literally watching my son move one step closer to death every day? I knew there were no guarantees. I knew I could very well be picking out a small coffin for my son in the all too near future. I knew I might have to explain to Alexcia one day why her baby brother didn't come home from the hospital. Still, I chose to always give God praise. Why? Because He gave Logan one more day. I was simply grateful for that one day.

I can promise you that practicing gratitude, especially when you're facing awful situations, is extremely challenging. I remember that initially, I had to make myself say the words, even when all I felt was insurmountable sadness. You might be thinking, *Wait a minute, I thought you had found all this deep faith in God's plan?* The answer is yes, I was absolutely developing a deep faith in God's plan for my life and my family's, but in no way is having that level of faith easy.

Deep faith can often come with what feels like a lot of sacrifice. It means actively choosing every day to be resilient and still professing your faith and trust in a divine plan even when your day doesn't go according to your plan. But practicing gratitude even when your plan hasn't been actualized becomes, with time, not just an act of faith but a lifeline that will secure you firmly in your spirituality and connection to a higher purpose. You will also, over time, acquire a perspective rooted in wisdom that surpasses the current issues you are grappling with.

I never once allowed myself to pray for a deceased donor. It just never sat right with me in my conscience. Instead, I started praying for God to speak into my heart and show me the way. I wanted Him to show me signs of what I needed to do to help my son. It was at this point that I decided to pursue living donation in Pennsylvania. Logan's primary hospital in Orlando was partnered with a well-renowned hospital in Pittsburgh, and through multiple inquiries, I found out they had a living donation program. We were hopeful once again. The Pittsburgh hospital approved Logan to be listed there as well, so now Logan could potentially find a donor from twice as many states.

As his parents, Skyler and I immediately jumped at the opportunity to be Logan's donors. We thought this was it, the miracle we'd been waiting for. We went through the screening process, but due to different factors, neither of us was approved to donate. Receiving this news was heartbreaking, but rather than let it crush me, I made it my mission to find Logan a living donor.

I took to social media and began sharing every step of Logan's journey. The ups and downs, the small victories and the scary moments. Every doctor visit and every test result, I shared it all. This became my therapy. I asked everybody and anybody who would listen to share his story in the hopes of finding a living donor. There was so much love and support that began pouring in from all parts of the country and even overseas.

I answered every inquiry that came in; in fact, there were quite a few individuals who stepped forward to be screened. Some were people we knew personally, and others were complete strangers and friends of friends. We were witness to the incredible love that can be found in humanity when people come together for a common cause. I felt so much gratitude. It is amazing what a support system can do, and at the core of it was my faith, our family, and our church.

One day, I received a text from a church sister; a horrible tragedy had occurred within her circle of friends. The surviving family member had been made aware of Logan's need for a liver, and they chose to fill out a directed donorship request should their deceased family member be a match for Logan. Again, this is another incredible act of love and generosity from a complete stranger. I was moved, overwhelmed by this great act of selflessness and sadness for this person's loss.

The following hours were gut-wrenching. I was at work, so I retreated to the breakroom and waited to hear from Logan's medical team. My brain was so overloaded with "what ifs" that my mind left my body. I just sat in still silence with my eyes closed for what felt like an eternity. I prayed quietly in my mind. Yet, never once did I ask God to make this deceased donor Logan's match. All I kept repeating was, "Let Your will be done. Let Your will be done. Let Your will be done." Then, after what felt like twelve hours (in actuality, it was about three), my phone rang. It was Logan's medical team. The donor was not a match.

I stared out the window of my work. It was such a gorgeous spring day. I was laser-focused on the trees, the swaying leaves, the warm colors of new life springing forth, and the warmth of the sun touching my skin. I was still in a state of prayer and fixating on the beauty of creation. All I wanted was for my baby to live.

I could have gotten angry, frustrated, and resentful that Logan's miracle had not manifested yet. But I didn't. I only prayed that Logan be granted mercy. How easy it would have been to become disheartened at that moment. How easy it would have been to slip into a state of bitterness, to have lost hope and belief that God was still present in Logan's life and mine. Logan had been fighting for so long. It was such a big battle, and he was so small and vulnerable.

With time, I would see that sometimes God's signs often present as unanswered prayers. What we might see as God not responding to our pleas is actually Him pushing us to turn in the direction we are meant to go, a path that ultimately ends in something much bigger than we ever imagined.

Soon after, my husband and I decided I should stay home with Logan and Alexcia full-time. This decision seemed completely counter-productive; after all, we were in over our heads in medical expenses. But we knew we could no longer rely on private childcare to handle Logan's needs.

All the while, Alexcia needed a lot of support as well. From the age of three and a half, she quietly and gracefully braved every doctor visit. She would take charge and help me comfort Logan while he cried during his blood draws, and she tolerated the long three-hour commutes to and from visits. I did my best to make doctor visits an opportunity for fun learning, and she processed the dire reality by becoming incredibly inquisitive about all things medical.

Alexcia had to grow up sooner than she should have. She was so hyper-aware that she started telling people, "Logan is my baby brother. He's very sick and needs a new liver." God bless her; she was a mini-me on a mission. She had come to understand all too clearly what death was. She was now five years old and knew Logan would die without a transplant. Alexcia needed stability and a lot of emotional support. On the other hand, Logan needed specific at-home medical care. He was now taking ten medications a day, some needing to be administered two or three times a day and timed exactly between scheduled meals and supplementation. We couldn't afford a full-time at-home nurse, so I had to stay home.

This was definitely not the Plan A we had intended. Then again, none of our plans had panned out. Our baby was sick; his liver disease was more advanced than his doctors had expected. Nine months had passed, and no donor had been found, and we were deep in credit debt as we struggled to support his medical costs. I'm sure some people probably thought I was making a big mistake leaving my job. Financially speaking, we were absolutely going out of the frying pan and into the fire. It made no logical sense to make this move, but God was pointing us in that direction. So we leaped.

On Easter day, a small number of family members gathered in our home. I hadn't told anyone except my husband about "the call that almost was" until that day. I knew it was a sensitive topic. No one said it, but everyone saw the horrible, deep jaundice that had permeated every part of Logan's body. We all saw the heavy discoloration of his skin, the xanthomas, and the scars and scabs from scratching. Most of all, no one could unsee the yellow that had now invaded every white part of his eyes.

I remember watching him that day. It was exactly one year after I had chosen to be baptized, a day that is synonymous with joy and elation for Christians around the world. At that moment it really sunk in: We were six months away from his second birthday, and I might not get to see him turn two later that year. I just watched him quietly. I was trying to soak in every little moment, every facial expression, every movement he made. I wanted to burn it into my mind.

Eleven days later, I got a call from Logan's Pittsburgh medical team. Logan had just gotten a new round of labs, and my first thought was, *Here we go; what's wrong now?* Usually, no news is good news. Whenever I'd get calls from his medical team after an exam, I'd steel myself up and get ready for another hospital admission, treatments, and new medications. I was all too well conditioned to brace for impact.

It was our nurse coordinator on the other line. "I have good news," she said... I didn't respond. I heard her. I just didn't know what to do with that statement. That was not a common phrase in our life. I did not allow myself false hope, so I waited for her to speak again. Then I heard, "Logan has a match."

I just about lost all feeling in my legs. My heart started racing, and then the tears came. I couldn't even muster words. I remember holding Logan in one arm and the phone in the other hand. I stood in the hallway, tears running down my face and trying to catch my breath. My husband was going in and out of the house doing yard work. He saw me and rushed over, bracing for the worst, but then realized they were tears of joy. We took a full breath for the first time in a long time. We stood in that hallway in a tight embrace with Logan and Alexcia, who had made her way over between us. Logan was set for surgery in four weeks on May 18.

Of course, just like everything else in this journey, this joyful event didn't go quite as planned. One week prior to surgery, Logan tested positive for RSV. He had to be put on hold status for two weeks minimum in order to be cleared of the virus. This meant he was officially ineligible for a donor. He could get skipped over in the transplant recipient line. He could lose his new liver. After all we had endured, was this virus going to be our Achilles heel? Was my child going to lose his chance to live because of this?

I knew these racing questions could have the power to cripple me. So I did what I knew would center me, what I knew would carry me through. I practiced my daily gratitude of prayer every day. I chose to be thankful for each day I had with Logan. I chose to be grateful that I could be home full-time to care for him when he needed me so much. I decided I would be grateful that I could enjoy watching him and his sister interact and share their lives.

As I captured every moment I could with so many pictures and videos, deep down, I knew what I was really doing. I was choosing to embrace and soak up every moment I had with Logan, especially if they were going to be some of the last I'd have with him. There were no guarantees he'd get to keep his donor. And most of all, there were no guarantees he'd ever get another chance.

Once again, another opportunity had presented itself, and I knew it could just as easily be taken away. How do you practice gratitude in times like this? I know that I did because I was fully surrendered to His will. By then, I firmly knew that our place in this world is but a temporary stop along the way. I knew that one more day with Logan was as much of a blessing as receiving a transplant. So, I was truly grateful.

How authentically are you practicing daily gratitude, regardless of the outcome? You have the ability to reset your focus from what you are lacking in life to what you are blessed with. And by doing that, you are not only finding peace in those moments but are redirecting your focus on what you can influence, what you can work on, and what you can improve. This is why I have come to appreciate the Serenity Prayer. The origin of it has much been argued, but most attribute it to American theologian Reinhold Niebuhr:

*God, give me the grace to accept with serenity the things that
cannot be changed, Courage to change the things that should be*

changed, and the Wisdom to distinguish one from the other.
Living one day at a time, Enjoying one moment at a time,
Accepting hardship as a pathway to peace, Taking, as Jesus did,
This sinful world as it is, Not as I would have it, Trusting that
You will make all things right, If I surrender to Your will, So that
I may be reasonably happy in this life, And supremely happy with
You forever in the next. Amen.

We waited a week to find out what would happen. It was awful. His donor was a living donor, which meant they could choose to be matched with the next person in line. That one week felt like a month. Finally, the news came in: Logan's donor chose to wait. Surgery was set for June 8th, his twenty-month birthday. God's miracle was only just beginning to unfold.

If there's one thing I want you to take away from this, it's that our Plan B can often be God's Plan A. His wisdom far surpasses our own, and He writes divergent paths in our lives that often feel like unanswered prayers. It takes a lot of courage to be willing to trust His will and not waver in faith. This means embracing what is unknown and walking forth with the unwavering belief that God will guide you down the right path. It means being thankful and grateful for what has been given to you, even when the picture you're looking at isn't what you expected.

This doesn't mean you won't ever feel disappointment, sadness, insecurity, or fear. No, it means you will have the strength to keep the faith in your greater purpose in this world, even in the face of difficult times. "For we live by faith, not by sight" (2 Corinthians 5:7). Know this: His plan for you is but another step away, and rest assured that He is guiding your steps with the clearest vision there is, even if that destination is unclear to you.

Leaning on God does not mean you're just going to sit back and let the chips fall where they may. It means being actively engaged in your spiritual growth and relationship with Him on a daily basis. For me, it meant giving up control and laying all my fears and pain at His feet. It meant diving into His word a little bit every day. It meant being open to receiving signs and nudges to take different paths. It also meant actively taking the time to pray and be thankful and grateful for the blessings I still had during the worst times.

It's always easy to be grateful when times are good, but the ability to practice gratitude even during our hardest times exemplifies trust in the greater divine purpose. It is the ultimate act of strength and faith against all adversity, which has the ability to shine the brightest light not just in your life but also in the life of those around you, in even the darkest of times.

HE MOVES MOUNTAINS

Soon enough we were in Pittsburgh and Logan's surgery day was finally here. Perhaps it would have been normal for me to be filled with worry that day, but instead it was a day of rejoicing. There was no fear, only joy. All I wanted was for Logan to have a second chance, and God had certainly delivered him that gift. The transplant went by with flying colors, there wasn't a single glitch, and it finished sooner than expected.

His surgeons were pleasantly surprised to be able to do a complete closure of the abdominal wall. Often, small children can only initially get a skin closure due to their body cavity being so small and the donated lobe being from an adult. This results in a second surgery after 12–18 months to then do a full closure. In Logan's case, the donated lobe was a perfect fit. Logan and I were expected to stay in Pittsburgh for six months before being sent home. His recovery was so seamless that we were sent home after only six weeks.

Returning home was a blessing, and our family was united once again. Life should have felt lighter, yet when Logan and I came home, we were quickly faced with another uphill battle. We had accumulated a mountain of debt from medical expenses. We were drowning. I went back to work as soon as I could, but it still wasn't enough. We were on the verge of losing our home, so we swallowed our pride and did something we never would have done otherwise.

We reached out to our community of friends and family and asked for help. It was incredibly uncomfortable. We were humiliated. We had always believed in working hard and making our own way no matter what. Life had humbled us immensely. We were embarrassed to go public with this information, but we knew we had reached our breaking point. We were going to lose our home and our vehicles. Friends stepped up to help us. Their generosity and kindness allowed us to stay afloat long enough to catch up on some expenses, but eventually, we still needed to sell our home.

Meanwhile, since Logan's return home, his story has been making its way across people's televisions and phones. The incredible story of him and his donor was inspiring and deemed newsworthy. What started as a local story quickly grew into national articles in *People* and on *Good Morning America*. We were soon contacted by producers from a national daytime talk show. They were genuinely interested in learning about Logan's story and our journey as a family.

Eventually they invited us to be guests on their show. We were honored and grateful for their graciousness, and the trip provided a short respite from the stress of having to sell our home. It was, after all, the first home we bought after getting married and the only home our children had known. Our host was incredibly kind and sensitive to our personal battle. Little did we know that she and her team would bless us beyond our imagining.

They arranged a surprise meeting with Logan's donor. Meeting her was like meeting an old friend, and seeing her meet Logan for the first time was such a beautiful moment. The blessing didn't end there. The host and producers gave us what we needed to wipe out our medical debt. In a split moment, we were finally okay. Our children could stay in their home, and we had a second chance at a bright future.

As I conclude this chapter, I hope that my words offer you an opportunity to reflect on your own path to this point in your life. Material wealth can buy us some pretty incredible things and experiences, no doubt about that, and it can also allow us to bless others who are in need. Along with your aspirations in career and financial prosperity, I pray that you will also take a leap of faith and jump onto the path of growing in your spirituality. Your faith is what will carry you, even during the darkest times. It will be what strengthens you and gives you the hope you need to keep persevering. It will give you peace when you need it the most.

Sharing our vulnerability, faith, and prayer is what opened the door to Logan's incredible recovery. It gave way for the outpouring of generosity from friends and strangers alike. It allowed us to bear witness to a glimpse of God's incredible tapestry and how we fit in it.

I encourage you to lean into your faith and be open to how your life can be insurmountably enriched through a personal relationship with God. Take the time to pray and learn to find your own voice as you do. There is no perfect way to pray. You can be on your feet, kneeling, in the temple of your choice, or in your car. It doesn't matter. He is alive in every atom that makes up our universe, and He will hear you. Choose to practice gratitude, even when it's hard. The more you focus on what you have in your life that is beautiful, loving, and joyful, the deeper and more steadfast your faith will become. Go forward with an open mind and heart, and know that God's plan will reveal itself in perfect time.

FIVE PRACTICAL STEPS TO HELP YOU GET STARTED ON YOUR JOURNEY OF FAITH

- **Pray Daily and Reflect**
  - Create space every day for prayer and reflection. Practice thanking God for His blessings and humble yourself to ask for His guidance and signs so that you may walk The Way and be witness to His holy presence.
- **Read the Word**
  - It doesn't matter what translation you read; take the time to read a bit of His word every day. Don't be afraid to ask questions and compare different translations. There is no set pace to read through the Bible. What's most important is allowing yourself the time to reflect on the passages you read and the lessons they teach. Ask yourself: *How can the message be applied to your daily life?*
- **Gratitude Journal**
  - Start journaling. You can do this in writing or you can vlog. You can choose to keep your reflections to yourself, or if you decide to take the next step in faith, you can share your thoughts with the world. You'd be

amazed how many people you can inspire and give hope to by being vulnerable and brave.

- **Find Your Tribe**
  - Seek out and build a network of support that appreciates your journey in faith. Find a community that encourages growth and welcomes questions. This is especially important because your journey of faith will be ongoing. You will have questions, and you want to ensure your community is open to helping you navigate your spiritual development.
- **Give Back**
  - Never turn down an opportunity to perform an act of kindness. You can donate to charities, volunteer your time to help an organization or a cause, or you can simply buy a meal for someone in need. Leading your life with a servant's heart will go further and impact more people than you know. No, not everyone will reciprocate or appreciate your acts. But giving back is not about reciprocity, gaining recognition, or profiting monetarily. It's about serving His creation, changing lives, and influencing even just one other person to follow suit.

Rasika Salva was born in Sri Lanka and raised in Belgium by Italian parents. She moved to the United States in 1993, bringing with her a rich tapestry of cultural experiences. Now settled in Ocala, Florida, Rasika is a devoted wife and mother of two. Fluent in English and Italian, she seamlessly blends her multicultural background into her daily life.

She has an extensive background in performance studies, focusing on dance, theater, and music. She has a bachelor's degree in Theater and Performance Studies from UC Berkeley and a master's degree in Theater Critical Studies from UC Los Angeles.

As the Director of Author Development for Game Changer

Publishing, Rasika helps industry professionals create massive impact as bestselling authors every day. She also owns The Graceful Warrior Boutique, which provides elegant and modest women's fashion. She authors a blog, *SimplyRasika,* dedicated to sharing insights and inspirations with women, wives, and mothers. When she's not helping new authors or running her business, Rasika loves spending time with her family and serving her church.

Shop at The Graceful Warrior Boutique
https://tgwboutique.com/

—

Facebook
@TGWBoutique

—

Instagram
@TGWBoutique

Follow *SimplyRasika* blog
https://simplyrasika.com/

—

Facebook
@SimplyRasika

—

Instagram
@SimplyRasika

Out of the Darkness and Into the Life

ESCAPING THE PRISON OF ABUSE

By Sharon Davis

Please join me on the adventure of life, in this case, mine. If any of you have been victims of abuse, neglect, deceit, and lies, you may recognize some familiarity with the hell that life can be until it finally becomes your own. It was when I learned I could escape the negative, suffocating, fear-based hold of others who initially had power over me—adding to my struggle to see through to find myself—that I finally learned to live. For me, it was decades before that door thankfully opened. First, my actions of learning steps to help myself, walking out, followed by the support and help of my work friends, therapists, grandmother, second husband, and his mother, who showed me women can survive.

I am so thankful I never lost that spark inside me that continues to burn. That place we reach when we stand looking into the eye of the enemy and know we will die here if we do not do something to save ourselves and those depending on us. In my case, the protective instinct went to my sibling before leaving home, as we survived the abuse of life together from age 3 to 18 when I married and left home. Unfortunately, we lost contact with each other in our struggle to survive, having led both of us to marry military men, who we thought would be protectors but turned into the Benedict Arnolds of our lives. For me, my spark directed me out of the marriage 17 years later, but my sibling's spouse passed three years ago, and she is still building the spark. I am so proud of the energy that flares more frequently now, finding the voice with her children who continue to attempt to control her life. My energy went to my children, stepsons, and now to my grandchildren and the people surrounding me personally and professionally. I opened my eyes one day and saw beyond the bubble I had been raised in—to know the hope of a limitless future with the love of my life beside me.

My life began in a northern California hospital. I was born premature, 4.5 oz. The doctor predicted if I lived, I would be "small." As a baby, my body went through the constant stimulation of a Neonatal Intensive Care Unit (NICU) with IV, blood transfusions, constant noise, and bright lights. If any of you have ever experienced sitting in the NICU with a newborn, you know better than I what that looks like. For the baby, science still does not know the impact on the central nervous system or on mental health in the future. Thankfully, I did not have vision issues or any noticeable brain damage, nor did I die as many premature babies did in 1950.

WHO WE ARE: MILITARY FAMILIES

My life as a Military Family Member and victim started at the age of 3 when the Monster was allowed to adopt us so he could provide insurance and other benefits for military families. I do not know if he told my mother to lie about our biological father or not, but I expected he would, as a power and control move over us.

Life changed at 3, going from a supportive and loving family unit to dependence on the family Monster in another part of the country. The only way to communicate was to write letters, which I could not, or make phone calls, which were too expensive. We were cut off from anyone outside the home until we went to school. From the little I can recall, life was good when he went out the door. Mother played with us and tried to see if we had what we needed and wanted. The atmosphere would change when he came in the door. At 5, I had to pull weeds in the garden while he watched, or I would be punished.

In her way, Mother did try to protect us by teaching us to be all covered up before we came out of the bedroom, though the Monster would walk around in boxer shorts allowing his penis to escape, and I never saw her intervene. It has taken years of therapy to see I was not the only one trapped on this horror ride.

When I turned 6, the physical abuse intensified, with me getting punished regardless of who broke the rules. When I turned 10, I had to babysit my 3-year-old brother. My mother started working on the base. I was assigned all household chores: cooking, cleaning, laundry, and groceries, which continued from the time I was 10 until I turned 18. Our brother did not mind, knowing he would never be punished. Punishments were given to me. All discipline was done by the Monster, with him having me get the switch and strip down to bare skin to receive punishment, leaving whelps too painful to sit down. If I cried, I was hit more; if I did not get a switch that satisfied him, he would get a bigger one. After age 8, he would start giving me restrictions. I do not recall if I took our brother's spankings or not, but I was given the responsibility of caring for him (the Monster's biological son).

In 1967, my mother told me lies about my father, and she would blame him for her actions. She accused him of the behaviors of my step-father. She never addressed my little naked body, running screaming down the hall to get away from the grown, naked man she had brought into my life as he chased me down the hall. I was taught to ignore, deny, endure, and no one would help me. Her response was, "We don't talk about that." After attending many hours of inpatient and outpatient treatment, I confronted her. I also drove to Iuka, Mississippi with my second husband (prior to our marriage) and my youngest son to confront the Monster. My mother stood in the door of her home and asked me why I was there. About that time I pushed her out of my way as I saw him beginning to run from the door. She continued to deny anything had happened and told me to get over it. The Monster ran out of the room, telling me to get away from him. I tried to confront him, but my mother was still supporting him. I had enough evidence and satisfaction that he was not a 12-foot man. He was a bully and an unconvicted pedophile Monster. Due to the statute of limitations being gone, I couldn't have him arrested and convicted. However, I did call the Child Abuse Hotline in Mississippi and advise them who he was, what he had done to me and if they had anyone in the area complain of the same behavior to look his way.

At age 11, the rapes started. I started my period at age 10, and I was developing early. I do not recall anything sexual before we moved to Japan. I do not know when he started coming into our rooms at night, but the memories coincide with our time living in Japan from third through sixth grade. My mother did not know about me getting on a bus to go to the hospital where he worked so he could sexually abuse me in his office. But she had to have known. Mom had to have seen our early reactions before we learned to be docile and endure the abuse.

I do know I emotionally lost my mother in Japan. Her body came home, but her spirit had left the building, and she was just a shell of herself until she had grandchildren. Shortly after arriving in Japan, she gave birth to my little sister, who was premature, like me. She was in an incubator and required oxygen, too, but due to the incompetence of the nurse who removed her oxygen and did not put it back, she passed. I recall the little box being boarded onto a plane to return to Ohio to be buried while we remained an ocean apart. When my mother lost the next baby, delivered stillborn, it took her spirit with it as she shut down. Finding out later about her diabetes was the last nail in the internal coffin she remained locked into until the day her body died. She became emotionally animated when my children were born. It was hard sometimes to hold back the jealousy I felt when I saw her love my children but not me.

THE SKILLS AND EXPERIENCES WE GAIN

In my experiences, I learned to be resilient and adaptable to circumstances that came my way. I learned about other cultures and developed a willingness to try new things. I learned to pack quickly and hold on tightly, as children's stuff would be the first to go if the household goods were overweight when moving. Education was less traditional than civilian counterparts being exposed to the history and culture of wherever we lived at the time. I learned acceptance of differences and respect for others in the places with in which we lived, more so if living off base.

I learned about finances and foreign exchange to be able to purchase goods when living abroad. I learned to cook the foods of the different areas we lived in, developing a broader palate than that of civilian family members. I was able to participate in cultural experiences in different countries, learning music, dance, and other entertainment. I learned how to survive on processed food when in places with delays in shipments and inconsistency at the commissary to be able to find desired foods. Whatever they had was all you could get. We ate a lot of SPAM. So, I learned to get by on what they had and not ask questions. I learned tolerance of authority with endless inoculations, just like the soldier in the family, following the rules and regulations and being checked regularly for multiple health conditions started in infancy.

The "don't ask, don't tell" policy applied to sexual preferences but also extended into other areas of the family by keeping hidden the affairs, domestic violence, and physical/emotional/sexual abuse. I learned to numb out, keep secrets, and accept blame. Those who rebelled were identified as the problem rather than the symptom of deeper problems. The process for getting help began with going through the soldiers' command and "telling on them," which was the biggest no-no of all. In my time as a military family member, the command's response to trouble with family, I found out in the last 25 years, was to move the family off post and ignore phone calls or pleas for help.

I suppressed my feelings about being abused at an early age as I followed my mother's example. She told me she was afraid we would starve if she left our abuser. Her mothering instincts were gone. I recall him screaming at her in their bedroom. He would drink his paycheck and leave us with little money to buy fresh food and staples, clothes, or toys. He had full control of us since my mother was unwilling to think outside the box without his permission.

Some may be wondering about the Monster and if his military service contributed to his behavior. The answer is yes. The military didn't create monsters; it provided an environment where they could thrive due to others' neglect of regulations and their disregard for the warning signs. Out of country, some soldiers would be like the natives in every behavior despite knowing it was illegal for them as an American citizen. Example: The mothers in the bars would have their young children available for a soldier to have for a few hours for money. Despite knowing their behavior was illegal I think today that is what contributed to the Monster raping us. He was drunk when he arrived home late at night, and he smelled like saki. He had been off base for a few hours.

As a Technical Sargeant (T/Sgt) he worked at the hospital on base as an x-ray technician. He had the rank of T/Sgt after 20 years, was physically unfit, and did not maintain his soldier bearing. He did not do his daily PT nor meet the height/weight requirements, but they kept him. To the military, he was not the Monster and he reminded us that no one would believe us if we tried to tell.

I often wondered at school if the other children lived as I did. I am sure they did then... as it still in happens in some military families. The message "If we wanted you to have a family, we would have issued you one" is still used today. Living in the military community made it hard to have friends and to see what other lives were like. My mother did not have friends, there were no play dates in our lives, and it was hard to get away from home to meet anyone other than at school. I took every advantage I could to learn and embraced every opportunity for fun.

I learned I had jumped into the fire when I married my first husband at age 18. He said I was his property on the day we bought our marriage license. I never had the luxury of coming into my sexuality by choice; first, the Monster took that from me, and then my first husband. I never had the fun of exploring those avenues of life and development and was well-trained to continue a life of abuse and domination. When my first husband found out about the abuse, his anger was that he was not my first sexual partner. Our dates consisted of going to drive-in movies or parking for my husband-to-be's sexual gratification. I did not realize I was being used.

I did not learn until years later about the dangers of familiarity and codependency, all of which come from dysfunctional or unhealthy relationships. I learned to endure plus survive, but I did not really *live* until decades later. Consequently, I was admitted to a 10-day inpatient treatment for Codependence in 1987. I learned about vulnerability and dangers in military families while being away from extended family for long periods. Our worst abuse happened when we were in Japan and in that time right before we went there.

The Monster transferred to Missouri after Japan but got orders to Vietnam a few months later. The family was forced to move off base and live in the community. My first time attending a civilian school was a shock. The students dressed differently and were behind where we were academically, which led to boredom, and it was hard to fit into the established cliques. Living in a small town with zero activities for children was a new experience for us having lived on base with thousands of other military and families. I graduated high school, married five days later, and got pregnant with my first son. The Monster returned from Vietnam and immediately transferred to Germany. He went unaccompanied. I had won a college scholarship, but my mother kept it from me.

I suspect my mother was as naive and uneducated as others in my family. The red danger flags were recognizable as she sought to meet her immediate need to escape rather than think about what she would be going into. She had done a similar thing in marrying my dad, as he was the brother of her oldest sister's husband, and they had been raised as cousins. Her father had been strict with his daughters.

Unlike my mother, after 17 years of abuse I decided I could not take any more. I had not been in treatment at that time, but the clarity of working outside of the home helped me see I needed to leave. Divorcing my abusive spouse and single-handedly raising a 12-year-old, 10-year-old, and a 5-year-old was a handful. I didn't let them know how hard it was. I had one pair of dress shoes to wear to work but used the extra money to keep my kids in shoes that fit them. I put cardboard inside my shoes when the soles wore out. I purchased the best garments for them I could afford but would sew a new outfit for myself as it was cheaper than buying clothes for me. Because I was a supervisor, I had a dress code I had to follow, and I did so by using my sewing, knitting, and crocheting skills.

At different times, each child left home before finishing high school. Years later, they aligned with their father, and the estrangement with me began. They returned to their abusive father to continue involving him in their lives, yet they shut the door on a relationship with me. My oldest followed his father's footsteps in joining the military, becoming a successful alcoholic (success being his ability to hide his actions from his superiors to make rank and climb the military ladder higher than his father had achieved) and an unfaithful husband. My daughter, the blamer, user, and manipulator, sees life for only what she can get out of it. My third chose the codependent role of staying for the children as he had seen me do initially. He had also seen the struggles and accomplishments that came after leaving. His voice said he would never abandon me; his actions took him back to his siblings and father with the encouragement of his wife. Prior to marriage, he had planned to take her back to Florida before the pregnancy occurred. The words I received, like blows from them, were worse than anything done by my parents, stepfather (the Monster) or husband. They deeply wounded my soul. Channeling this pain into helping others find healing and balance—something I've struggled to achieve with my own children—fuels my passion.

I am so thankful my ex-husband did not keep me homebound, or I would have died within whatever walls he had imprisoned me. He used his money for alcohol and women, which led us to need an additional income, so I was allowed to work outside the home. Obtaining a federal civil service job at age 22, being on base, and starting to meet other people, plus having the opportunity to learn, was the first real lifeline I received. I started volunteering to learn what was available to military and civilian workers. My mother had not tried to learn anything or take any steps to help her situation. Even in my accomplishments, when I asked her to come to see me in my first presentation to the FEW (Federally Employed Women), she made me my outfit and delivered it to me, but she did not stay to watch my achievements. Later with my first college degree, she did not come to witness or celebrate my accomplishments. She never encouraged me to advance up the career ladder. She was only a GS-6 on the pay scale, so I held myself back from promotions so as not to embarrass her. When I left the government to pursue college, I was a GS-6. When I returned with a master's degree and a license to practice, I was hired as a GS-11. I had shed the idea of holding myself back.

I am thankful for the times my maternal grandmother made me feel like I could do anything I wanted. She taught me what love looks like, developed my desire for knowledge, inspired the parts inside me that never died, and pushed me to keep going even when I wanted to stop. I am thankful to my mother for teaching me to sew and craft, as both have served as salvation, financially and mentally. The school was a haven from home, and though I had difficulty with reading (dyslexia and lazy eye), I was able to learn through demonstration and observation and was rewarded with the goal of accomplishment. I struggled, but I persevered. Those were the stable parts of my foundation: the hell from which I crawled out from, vowing never to go back, and my journey forward, which will continue until the day I die.

I met my father when I was 47. After much research and sending letters to my relatives, my grandma (my mom's mother) helped me find him. She said she couldn't keep the secret and felt I should know him. He had been visiting her all my life. I drove to Arkansas to the address where he was visiting. He told me to get back in the car and follow him to the gas station. He was upset that I was driving on tires with steel belts sticking out and my wiper blades were worn down. He paid for all of the above despite me telling him I couldn't pay today but would pay him back.

I knew him immediately when our eyes met. I was elated as I finally felt whole. My father's hair was completely white at 18, which helped me accept the white hair I had hated. I have now come to be grateful for it since it gave me that connection to him. I was named after one of his sisters. I look like him which may play into my mother's attitude towards me. His birthday is a day before mine. We both love Christmas, and he loved the same foods I did. I sat and talked to him for 12 hours that first day, and he opened up, telling me to ask him anything I wanted to know. I am angry at my mother for the lies and being separated from the truth til 1986; look at all the years we were denied. My father and I only had three years together before he passed.

THE CULTURAL DIVIDE

Culture plays a significant role in military organizations, impacting strategy, planning, training, and overall effectiveness in war. Military culture is deeply ingrained and can influence member's actions unconsciously. Understanding military culture is challenging due to external factors that shape and distort it.

The cultural divide begins with the ranking system and how families and soldiers are treated based on their rank status. Within the ranks, the cultural divide comes through in favoritism. The enlisted and commissioned officers had designated places for each to go, with penalties for any violations or disrespect of the military culture. The divide between the sexes has all the power on the part of the male or female soldier, with the soldier being accountable for whatever was known to be happening in the family.

The division between military and civilians has broadened the misinformation on both and the differences in freedoms in being on or off base. Even away from the base, the military is always under the microscope of the powers to uphold the integrity of the military—and do not get caught if you deviate as there were consequences of loss of rank and court martial.

The divide in the relocations, particularly out of country, depends on where you go and that country's view toward the U.S. Some countries view the U.S. Military as an invader and do not want them there, while others are appreciative and inviting. This impacts the family and is much harder when living off base and in the communities.

The Vietnam War marked a dramatic shift in how civilians perceived the military's role as warriors and protectors. Amid protests, shaming, name-calling, and blame, the public failed to recognize that the men and women were merely following orders from their commander-in-chief, not choosing to enter another country to kill or die. This disconnect has continued with the wars that followed as there was a drift away from patriotism, even within the military.

HOW I BEGAN TO HELP VETERANS

I began working on a Navy base at age 22. I stayed until I was 37. I worked for the Naval Reserves on the same base for four years and 13 years for the largest inland training base in charge of producing all the naval training materials. I began volunteer work in a substance abuse program for active duty, a volunteer Equal Employment Counselor and volunteer Federal Women's Program Manager, which opened the door to learn about the internal workings of the military to access services. Being able to work on base provided an essential part of helping the active duty soldiers in my earlier years of employment on base in Millington, Tennessee; I am able to connect to veterans of today. Being a federal employee provided an insight into the world outside the home and the daily issues of soldiers and their families. With years of education, working at Federal Express at night and going to graduate school during the day to obtain my first master's degree and licensure required, I finally landed a position at the Veterans Administration Medical Center in Memphis as a Licensed Professional Counselor to hospitalized veterans and active duty service members. Like many from military families, the heart is always with the military and remains after time served. Paying it forward and helping others was invaluable in connecting with me. Working with active duty added to the foundation and increased my passion for being there for soldiers and their families. This continues as I do individual sessions with veterans, and I'm always on the lookout for what can be learned and taught to them. With the technological age comes the necessity of learning how to use the internet to reach more veterans and their families. I worked at Fort Campbell for six years, and I am presently in private practice treating veterans and families dealing with mental health issues due to having been deployed.

WHAT BEING LIMITLESS AND SUCCESSFUL MEANS TO ME

Always look for a way around, over, or through, and never give up. The path is rough, with many turns and twists, but you keep putting one foot in front of the other and figure out how to make it happen. It means constant problem-solving to find what can be done and letting go of the restraints others impose. Keeping the passion to learn how to protect oneself and others is a driving force, as is the desire to educate and teach others how to defend themselves.

In conclusion, we have no control over our birth or death date, but the dash in the middle is where we live. Early life is often hampered by the choices of others, good or bad, but the path of the dash is limitless and all about finding what is needed and working hard to use what you have learned to reach your stars.

I wish all of you success in your journey to the stars. In the world of abuse survivors, it is extremely hard to find someone who will talk or write and be willing to put their story of survival out in the universe. In 1986, at the beginning of my treatment, I looked diligently for articles, textbooks, books, workshops, and conventions to learn more about myself. I am now one of those who is willing to talk, write, or meet with other survivors to attempt to help them open the door to a better life.

By the time this book is published, I will have designed and made available a pilot workshop and will announce the details in November. I'll have more information about what I can do to help those who are struggling with similar issues and get myself in the position to talk to others online, via Zoom, etc. You will receive a gift for showing up, but you need to register early as I have only 200 seats available.

I can be contacted through my website (see link below). Thanks for being a part of my journey through life to reach my brass ring with the star on it!

Sharon Davis was originally employed as a Civil Service Federal Employee and after 17 years of employment she decided to resign to attend college for the first time in her life. She obtained a part time job at Federal Express so she could go to college full-time. Loving to fly, she flew as a jump seater in the cockpit for five years.

She worked at several companies in customer service before becoming an Addiction Services Team Supervisor at Frayser Family Medical Center. Sharon was then hired by the Veteran's Administration Medical Center to design and implement an outpatient intensive treatment program for the Substance Abuse Treatment Ward so she went back to Federal Civil Service for six years. She decided to go back to college to obtain a master's degree in social work as the VAMC wouldn't recognize an LPC for the same grade as an LCSW even though she was doing same job.

Sharon now holds the following degrees and certificates: Certificate of Addiction Services, bachelor's degree in Professional Studies (eating disorders, codependence, and sexual abuse), two master's degrees in Counseling (as a Licensed Professional Counselor), and Social Work (as a Licensed Clinical Social Worker).

While living in Memphis, Sharon's spouse's 29-year-old son committed suicide. Her husband had lived there all his life but understandably couldn't handle being there any longer with all the memories. They moved to Clarksville, Tennessee in 2009.

Sharon went to work at Fort Campbell as a counselor for six years. She decided to retire in 2014 and has been in private practice since. When COVID hit, she moved her private practice into her home to utilize the Telehealth platform to treat Army veterans with mental health or Post Traumatic Stress Disorder for VAMC and has been there ever since.

The first link below is where you may register for part 2 of my chapter you have read. I will have the rest of my story up to today and the steps I made to be telling my story. Once you register and watch my story, you will receive a free gift I made for you that helped me in the journey I am on. I dedicate this to all victims of the abuse, attempting to get out of or still in their abusive situation. Please don't give up.

For more information or to contact Sharon
https://sharonldavislcswlpc.com/

—

Sharon Davis, Consultant
Facebook
https://www.facebook.com/profile.php?id=100066682869490

Sharon Davis
Facebook
https://www.facebook.com/SharonDavis4/

—

Instagram
https://www.instagram.com/meetsharondavis/

Beyond Clarity

UNLOCK THE FREQUENCY OF MIRACLES
WITHIN YOU

By Zhivka Hristova

Welcome to my chapter! Thank you for opening this book and reading my message. I will share with you my deepest truths, my personal and professional journey, and how my gifts transform the lives of many human beings.

I also welcome you to look within and ask yourself: *Do I want to be the one who is healed, abundant, and happy?*

I am a woman who has traversed the complexities of life, from deep struggles to profound breakthroughs. My journey has taken me from the depths of personal despair to the heights of spiritual and financial freedom. I am a Quantum Mindset Coach and Light Language Healer, committed to guiding women through their own transformations.

My journey was born out of necessity and an unyielding desire to break free from the chains of my past. I was confronted with hardships that could have broken me, but instead, I chose to look within, harnessing the power of quantum energy to clear my trauma and rediscover my true self. This journey led me to the gift of Multidimensional Light Language Healing, a powerful tool that I now use to help others.

I wrote this chapter because I believe that every woman has the potential to create her best life and business. The quantum field is available to all of us, and we can access limitless possibilities by tapping into it.

My goal is to share the insights and tools that have transformed my life so that you can step into your power and create the life you desire, too.

This chapter is for the woman who is ready to take control of her life and who is tired of being held back by past traumas and limiting beliefs. It is for the woman who knows she is meant for more but needs guidance on how to access her full potential.

I've walked the path from struggle to success. I've experienced firsthand the power of quantum energy and light language healing. I've transformed my life, and I've helped countless other women do the same. My story is proof that no matter where you start, you have the power to change your reality.

In this chapter, you'll discover how to connect with your higher self, clear the traumas of your past, and harness the quantum field to create the life and business of your dreams. You'll learn practical steps to elevate your consciousness, set boundaries, and attract the right people and opportunities into your life.

My hope is that after reading this chapter, you will feel empowered to take action.

I want you to recognize the immense power within you and begin to use it to create the life you've always desired!

I truly hope you will start your journey of self-healing, knowing that you are not broken but rather ready to rise to your full potential.

Let's begin this transformative journey together, starting with the story of how I found the courage to look within and change my life.

MY ORIGINS STORY: AWAKENING THE FIRE WITHIN

Let me take you on a journey—a journey marked by trials, self-discovery, and an unwavering pursuit of authenticity. My hope is that my story ignites a spark within you, encouraging you to embrace your uniqueness and chase your dreams with unshakable resolve.

Life is far from a straight road; it's a winding path with sharp turns, steep climbs, and unexpected detours. My story is one of resilience, of pushing forward even when the odds seem insurmountable.

Like many, I've had moments when it felt like conformity was the only way forward. The crushing weight of expectations—from family, society, and even my own self-doubt—bore down on me. But in those moments of doubt, I learned to pause, to silence the noise around me, and to listen closely to the whisperings of my heart.

You are inherently beautiful, capable, and worthy. Your dreams and passions matter—they are the guiding stars illuminating the path to your most authentic self.

I, too, found myself standing at the crossroads, torn between the desires of others and the quiet call of my own aspirations. Society beckoned me toward predefined roles, urging me to fit into molds that felt foreign to my spirit. Yet, deep inside, I knew I was meant for something different, something more. Choosing to honor my dreams wasn't easy— it required courage, defiance, and a willingness to step into the unknown. But I did it, and I embarked on a path that felt authentically mine.

My journey was not without its share of stumbling blocks and uncertainties. I faced moments of crippling self-doubt, encountered setbacks that seemed impossible to overcome, and heard the echoes of naysayers questioning my choices. But through it all, I discovered a profound truth: Resilience is not born from comfort but forged in the fires of adversity. Every setback and challenge became a stepping stone on my path to growth.

Growing up in a middle-class family in Varna, a vibrant city on the shores of the Black Sea in Bulgaria, I was a young rebel at heart, constantly challenging societal norms. The sun-drenched beaches, where tourists enjoyed a freedom that seemed worlds away from my own life, ignited dreams within me. I dreamed of a life beyond the oppressive shadows of Communism and the heavy hand of the Soviet Union.

My first taste of the world beyond the Iron Curtain came at 14 during a school trip to Russia. The experience was eye-opening, but it was a visit to my sister in Germany a few years later that truly stoked the flames of my wanderlust. I glimpsed the vast canvas of the world, and I longed to paint my own story across it. That hunger for exploration took root deep within me, and I knew there was no turning back.

For many years, I felt like I was running—not just from the physical confines of my homeland but from something deeper, something intangible. It took me years, well into adulthood, to realize that I wasn't just fleeing my surroundings; I was escaping a profound sense of not belonging within my own family. I was different, a square peg in a world of round holes, yearning to carve out a life on my own terms, to make my own choices, and to learn from my own mistakes.

My journey began in a place of deep inner turmoil. I was trapped in a cycle of pain and self-doubt, feeling disconnected from my true self. It wasn't until my forties that I truly began to turn inward, seeking the answers that had eluded me for so long. I immersed myself in the study of mindset and quantum energy, diving deep into the layers of trauma that had held me back. Through this transformative process, I received the gift of light healing, a powerful modality that reconnected me with my higher self.

We all have moments when we forget who we truly are. Society, trauma, and our own fears cast a shadow over our vision, obscuring the truth. But beneath it all, we are powerful, beautiful beings capable of extraordinary things. It's time to strip away the layers, to reconnect with your higher self, and to awaken the limitless potential that lies within you.

WHAT IS LIGHT LANGUAGE QUANTUM HEALING?

Quantum healing is about awakening to a reality beyond the physical.

My body is a conduit, and the light codes I channel with my hands are from Higher Vibrational Beings and Divine Sources. I work only with the highest possible frequency as I connect directly with Angels Realm and Holy Spirit! It always comes from the light in a way that aligns with your soul to support you on your path. It bypasses your logical mind, and you will receive the light codes through to your heart, consciousness, and soul. It's best to allow yourself to come into a space of love and gratitude.

It is multidimensional healing and it works on cellular levels, vibrational levels, and physical and subtle energy levels. You will receive healing exactly where your body, mind, and soul need it at the time. It will awaken the memory in your DNA.

It will help you break free from the conditioned patterns of the logical mind and activate your intuition. It is a powerful way to connect more deeply with the Divine Source and ascend on your higher path, moving through blocks and limiting beliefs that are holding you back in the old 3D reality. And support your ascension into the fifth dimension. Raising your vibration and consciousness to a higher level.

Higher consciousness is not an abstract concept; it's the deepest part of you that knows the truth about who you are and what you're capable of. When you align with this higher state of being, you unlock the ability to manifest your desires and live the life you've always dreamed of.

With Light Codes I can reprogram your energetic field for a specific purpose like the flow of love, abundance, vitality, and creativity. Light Codes transmission is a coding of the energy that works deep beyond the levels of the conscious or subconscious mind to repair or rewire energetic patterns that negatively affect your day-to-day life and hold you back on your soul-aligned path.

SHED THE PAST TO RECEIVE THE FUTURE YOU WANT

The power to create your life is within you!

But first, you must shed the layers of past pain and conditioning that have kept you from seeing your true self. This journey is about putting yourself first, loving yourself for who you are, and opening your heart to receive the abundance the universe has to offer.

Your heart is the most powerful energetic organ you have and it's directly connected with the quantum field. We naturally close our hearts to protect ourselves, but that also stops us from attracting positive opportunities. When your heart is open radiating love and positivity, you become a magnet for the abundance you desire.

Healing isn't about fixing yourself—because there's nothing wrong with you. It's about remembering who you are, setting boundaries, and allowing yourself to grow into the person you were always meant to be.

For example, when I was working with Kate, who experienced deep childhood trauma, the generational pattern of abuse, and a toxic relationship that was affecting her whole body, She had experienced constant back pain, heart problems, and bad eyesight for 20 years and was on medication for depression and anxiety.

When I assessed her energy and cleared all stagnant energies in all her body chakras and energy fields, her health improved significantly.

She no longer needed her medication, and her eyesight improved so much that she used a weaker prescription for her eyeglasses. She lost weight (28 pounds). As she became an expert in her field, her business started to flourish with new connections, clients, and precise offers. Her creativity was enhanced to such an extent that she wrote a book and a new program that had never been written or published online or offline before.

By choosing to heal herself, she is healing her family lineage and opening the doors for her children's future prosperity. Is that not the best gift you can give to your kids? It's priceless!

And this was just the beginning of Kate's journey after she found her purpose in helping women to align with their innate worth and self-love to manifest with ease their soul mates—something she didn't even know that she was meant to do!

HOW TO START TRANSFORMING YOUR LIFE

Transformation starts with choosing to change, letting go of your old identity, and knowing yourself through increased self-awareness.

When you start to look at yourself from the outside, you begin to see who you truly are, and you recognize your triggers and shadows.

It is a process that you consciously decide to follow. It is your choice to open yourself to self-knowledge, self-love, self-worth and connect deeply with your innate skills.

Take the time to set boundaries, live in gratitude, and shift your mindset from scarcity to abundance.

Your thoughts create your reality, and when you elevate your vibration, you attract the right situations and people into your life.

The highest vibrations are *authenticity, love,* and *gratitude.*

When you live in these states, you become a powerful force for positive change in your life.

Don't let the fears based on your past experiences—like fear of success or fear of failure—hold you back!

Your limiting beliefs—*I am not good enough, I can't have everything, I don't deserve to be happy,* or *I am not worthy of success*—are the reason you subconsciously self-sabotage. When you let go of what does not serve you anymore, you will see how your life begins to unfold in beautiful and unexpected ways. Your vibration is rising, and you will manifest with ease and attract the right people and opportunities aligned with your desires.

When you unlock your quantum powers, you can gain:

- **The power to expand time.** You can do more in less time than ever before without adding stress to your life.
- **The power to experience "sustained fire."** This will keep you operating at your highest energy level throughout even the longest, most challenging days
- **The power to partner with the energy of the Universe.** This will allow you to accomplish your goals more easily and fulfill your dreams.
- **The power to expand and express your creativity.** You'll be able to do this without sacrificing your daily responsibilities.
- **The power to almost magically attract everything you need.** You'll easily manifest the money, the right people, and all the resources you need to move your projects forward and achieve the level of success you're striving for.

EIGHT EASY STEPS TO UNLEASH YOUR FREQUENCY OF MIRACLES

1. **Find a quiet space.** Find a quiet and comfortable place where you won't be disturbed. It could be a cozy corner of your home, a peaceful spot in nature, or any place where

you feel at ease and can fully immerse yourself in introspection.

2. **Gather your materials.** Prepare a notebook or journal, along with a pen, to jot down your thoughts and reflections.

3. **Set an intention.** Before you begin, take a moment to set an intention for this exercise. Consider telling yourself something like *I intend to delve deeply into my past experiences of awareness and gain valuable insights from them.*

4. **Recall a moment of high awareness.** Close your eyes and take a few deep breaths to center yourself. Recollect a time when you felt immensely aware. It could be a memory of a significant event, a serene walk in nature, or a period of intense concentration and clarity.

5. **Observe without judgment.** Reflect on this moment without passing any judgment. Simply observe the thoughts, feelings, and sensations you experienced during that time. Pay attention to how your body feels, the emotions that arise, and the thoughts that occupy your mind.

6. **Describe the moment in detail.** Write a thorough and detailed description of this moment. Encompass as many sensory details as possible. Describe what you saw, heard, smelled, tasted, and touched during that experience. Try to encapsulate the essence of the moment in your own words.

7. **Reflect on the impact.** Contemplate how this moment of heightened awareness affected you. Did it alter your perspective? Did it lead to any significant insights or realizations? How did you emotionally respond to this experience?

8. **Relate to consciousness and awareness.** Consider how this moment ties in with the concepts of consciousness and awareness. How did your level of awareness influence your experience during that particular moment? What did you discover about your own consciousness through this experience?

MY LIFE-CHANGING WEALTH LIGHT CODES METHOD

With my unique Wealth Light Codes Method, I help women like you who want to skyrocket their businesses with the power of energy and transform all areas of your life!

Let's shed the old and step into a new identity, leaving behind past trauma, outdated beliefs, and generational patterns.

My method is truly unique—you'll feel an instant shift after just one session with me!

By accessing your Akashic Records, I'll pinpoint the exact origins of your limiting beliefs and energetically clear them, freeing you from subconscious self-sabotage.

At the same time, I'll transfer your own light codes to release stagnant energy and emotions, helping you move forward on your journey. It will also accelerate your body's self-healing process and restore it to its original blueprint, bringing an end to pain, anxiety, and depression.

I will help you open your third eye, connect you to your higher self, and open your heart to receive the abundance you so deserve!

HOW YOU CAN CONNECT WITH YOUR OWN QUANTUM POWERS

With my extraordinary gifts and abilities as an activator, I will also connect you with your spirit guides and your own gifts to tap into the quantum power yourself. My most potent superpower is my ability to ignite greatness in *you!*

1. Quantum fields have been known about for some time now, but it's only very recently that a few of us—and I'm one of them—have been figuring out ways to bring these quantum powers into daily life in ways that allow you to step into much, much larger possibilities for your life. Quantum powers are based on the recognition that we not only live in the universe, but the universe lives in us. With a turning of the mind and the psyche, one can tap into this great

universal, loving, creative force and use it for the
manifestation of healing and greater possibilities.

2. What *shifts* can you expect after tapping into the power of
quantum healing and endless energy? By tapping into the
power of quantum healing and endless energy, you will
experience increased bursts of inspiration and creativity,
allowing you to accomplish more at optimum energy levels.
You will develop profound healing and energizing
techniques to more clearly *feel* issues that arise in your body,
intuitively knowing how best to approach them. You will
come to know and experience yourself as deeply loved and
cherished. You're empowered, you're affirmed, and your
fullness is ignited.

3. The first step you can take right now to tap into the
quantum power is to connect with your quantum guides.
Write a letter to this all-knowing, all-loving spiritual partner
—whether you call it the entelechy, God, Aegis, or just
spiritual guides:

4. *Dear spiritual guides, how can you help me now? I
feel*_____
And insert whatever you feel. Then, respond back as the
spiritual guides, as a stream of consciousness. Listen deeper,
and if you get words, say them out loud. As you write with
your great, loving friend, know that so much potential is
being developed in you.

The message of this chapter is simple:

You have the power to create your best life and business. By tapping
into the quantum field and embracing your higher self, you can overcome any obstacle and achieve your dreams.

Thank you for taking the time to read my story. My hope is that you
feel inspired and empowered to start your own journey of self-healing.
The possibilities are endless when you tap into your true potential!

Next steps? Begin your journey today. Embrace self-healing, and if
you're ready to take your transformation to the next level, I invite you to
join me in my 12-week coaching program, "Beyond Clarity 1-2-1." In

this private encounter, you'll get personal healing and guidance from me as we work together to create the life and business you've always dreamed of.

Don't wait. Go to my website (see link below) and book!

Zhivka Hristova is a Conscious Success Mentor, Akashic Record Consultant, Light Codes Healer, and Activator. She pioneered the Wealth Light Codes Method, an innovative fusion of 5,000-year-old hermetic principles with modern insights from Psychotherapy, Neuroscience, Epigenetics, and Quantum Physics. Her work goes beyond addressing mindset and beliefs, focusing on aligning energetic essence for profound transformation.

Zhivka empowers individuals to unlock their potential, embrace their authentic passions, and manifest their dreams effortlessly, guiding them toward a life of abundance, prosperity, and lasting legacy. Ready to step into your role as a Conscious Creator? Reset, Master your Past, Rewire your Mind, and Redesign your Future! Let's align your life with your soul's true purpose.

Zhivka is committed to raising humanity's vibration. She worked with many people to uplevel their lives by uncovering the truth of who they are to the core, creating profound results in their businesses and relationships.

For more information or to contact Zhivka, go to her website
www.zhquantummind.com

—

Instagram
https://www.instagram.com/mindset.recodecoach?igsh=
MXhvYm9jbXh2ZTMwdQ%3D%3D&utm_source=qr